# PARADISE
# GARDENS

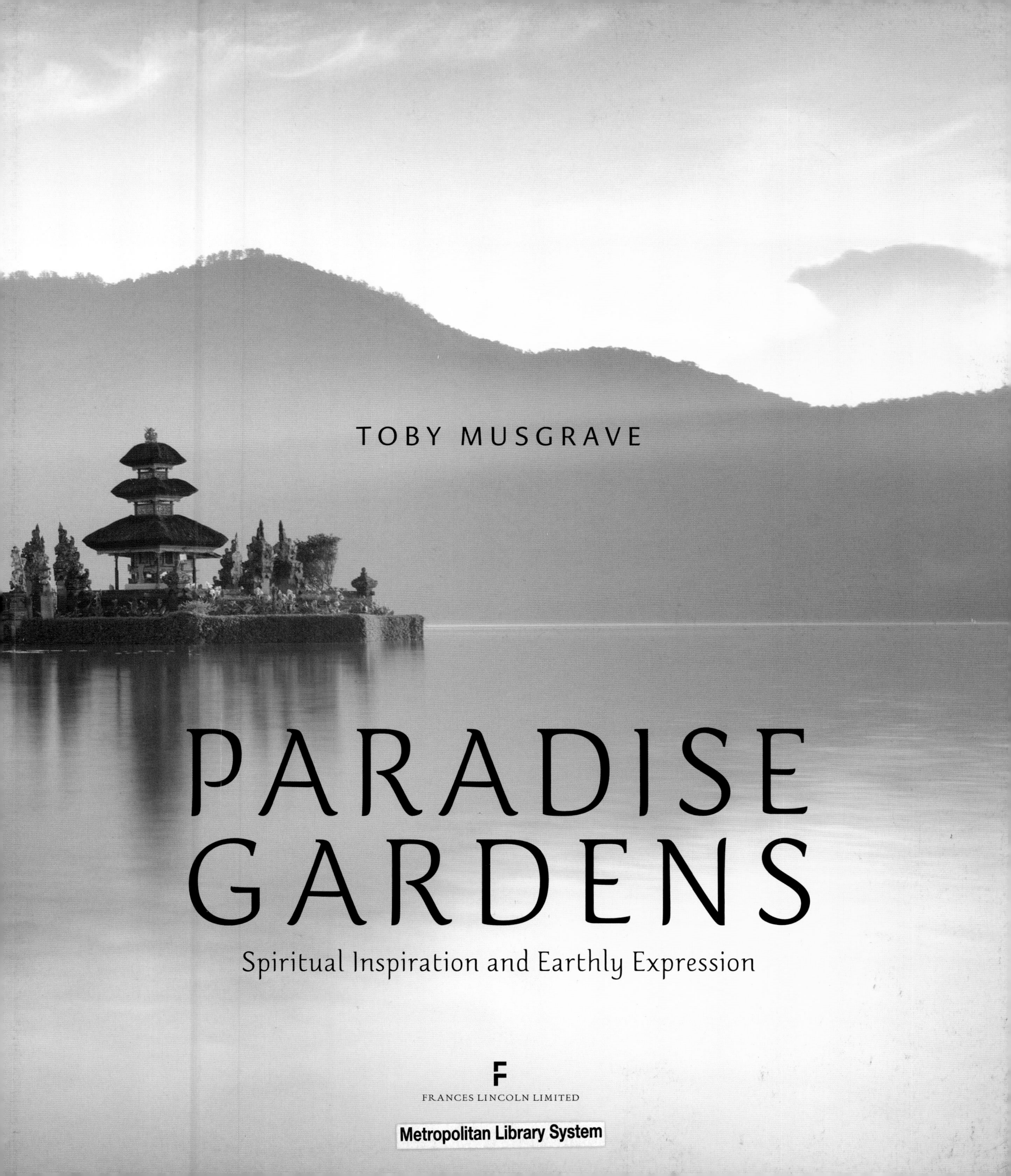

TOBY MUSGRAVE

# PARADISE GARDENS

Spiritual Inspiration and Earthly Expression

**F**

FRANCES LINCOLN LIMITED

Frances Lincoln Limited
74–77 White Lion Street
London N1 9PF
www.franceslincoln.com

A catalogue record for this book is
available from the British Library.

978 0 7112 3653 0

Printed and bound in China

1 2 3 4 5 6 7 8 9

Commissioned and edited by Jane Crawley
Picture research by Giulia Hetherington
Designed by Lewis Hallam Design

HALF TITLE
In Norse mythology Yggdrasil was a sacred ash tree.
This World Tree and Tree of Life connected all realms
of the Universe.

TITLE PAGE
The *pelinggih meru* or pagoda-like tiered roofs towers
of Ulun Danu temple on Bratan lake, Bali, Indonesia
are symbolic of the mystic and holy Mount Meru.

PAGES 4 AND 5
Water and rock are religio-symbolic cornerstones
of the Japanese garden and here at *Mōtsū-ji* temple
in Hiraizumi, Iwate Prefecture the wreathing of
mist adds an ethereal dimension.

# CONTENTS

# Introduction

Since the dawn of civilisation and throughout the world a diversity of distinct belief systems has arisen. Some have disappeared while others are still practised. Their doctrines vary widely but, irrespective of when or where, an article of faith that unites them all is a reverence for nature, the use of plants as emotive emblems imbued with symbolism and, in most cases, paradise gardens. Gods and goddesses have been and are revered as the providers of plants useful to mankind's existence. According to Ancient Greek mythology it was Demeter who gave us wheat and Dionysus, the grape, and both Jews and Christians consider the date palm and olive to be 'God-given'. Other plants with no practical use were and are imbued with religious meaning and symbolism and used for ceremonial and ritualistic purposes: the sea daffodil of the Minoans, the mistletoe of the Celts, the 'three friends of winter' of Buddhists, the rose of Sharon (probably *Gladiolus italicus*) of Abrahamic religions. Divine nature and gardens appear both in creation myths and, as a reward to the faithful, as delightful afterlife destinations. The hereafter of Elysium in Greek myth and that promised to Pure Land Buddhists are idyllic natural landscapes, while Jannah of Islam and the Aztec Tlolocan are described as paradisiacal gardens. So too are the locations of creation myths associated with Abrahamic Eden and Sumerian Dilmun. Such divine gardens inspired earthly paradises, and gardens imbued with a religio-significance were made by cultures as diverse as those of Mesopotamia, Ancient Egypt and Rome, Islam and by Buddhists in both China and Japan. Certain of these religio-inspired gardens and forms of idealised nature subsequently influenced secular garden fashions, including the eighteenth-century English landscape garden.

These are a few 'tasters' of what will be explored in the following chapters. But the very fact that so many different religions so geographically and chronologically disparate share

the same themes begs the question 'why?' At a biological, species level *Homo sapiens* and his immediate ancestors developed certain traits – a large brain and hence high intelligence, the ability to use tools (which requires an understanding of causality), spoken language and symbolic communication, the realisation of 'self', the concepts of morality, group living and, importantly, continuity – that led to the development of religious behaviour. The earliest surviving evidence for religious thought is the ritual interment of the dead, an act that represents an awareness of life and death, while the inclusion of grave goods signifies a concern for the dead that transcends daily life and possibly embraces the concept of an afterlife.

LEFT This fifth-century BCE Greek terracotta relief from the Sanctuary of Persephone at Locri Epiziferi in Italy shows a male figure carrying ripe bunches of grapes on the vine making an offering to, presumably, Persephone who is holding two ears of wheat and reaching out to accept the offering.

ABOVE Many Ancient Greek deities were assimilated by the Ancient Romans. This first-century AD mosaic uncovered in Pompeii shows Demeter who was known by her Roman name of Ceres.

Archaeological evidence from the cave of Sima de los Huesos in the Atapuerca mountains of northern Spain dates this practice to at least 350,000 years ago and our extinct ancestor *Homo heidelbergensis*. While no evidence of this age has yet been discovered to confirm the hypothesis, it is a rational assumption that our near ancestors also revered and worshipped the very environment on which their lives depended. Until the Agricultural Revolution some 10,000 years ago when mankind settled down to become a village farmer, humans were hunter-gatherers who subsisted on the flora and fauna they encountered during their migrations. Plants alone supplied, among other things, the raw materials for shelters, heat and light, weapons and utensils, food and medicines. And when we jump forward to 58,000 BCE we do find evidence that points to plant reverence by *Homo neanderthalensis* (Neanderthal man). Pollen analysis of soil samples taken from around the skeleton of burial Shanidar IV discovered in the Shanidar cave in the Zagros mountains of Iraqi Kurdistan is indicative that plants, or at least flower heads, were buried with the body of a male aged 30 to 45.

Moreover, all of the eight species identified and which included common yarrow (*Achillea millefolium*), cornflower (*Centaurea cyanus*), feverfew (*Tanacetum parthenium*) and grape hyacinth (*Muscari neglectum*) are known to have medicinal properties. This suggests that the deceased may have been some sort of medicine man, that the plants were placed with him in respect of his shamanic status and that the plants themselves were revered for their therapeutic qualities.

Early man would undoubtedly have been grateful for nature's munificence, would have attuned his behavioural patterns with the various cycles of nature, would have respected that not everything in nature was beneficial and would have failed to understand nature's violent and sometimes destructive forces. Nature was therefore probably perceived as a dynamic and powerful force beyond the control of man and it is completely understandable that something so mysterious and ubiquitous should have been personified and deified. 'She' was contrary — both munificent and harsh, a creator and destroyer — and there can be little doubt that she was respected, revered and worshipped in the hope that she

LEFT This voluptuous ivory figurine, the Venus of Hohle Fels, may represent an earth or mother goddess. Dated to around 40,000 years old the piece is considered to be the oldest example of human figurative prehistoric art.

RIGHT The painting of various animals depicted on the walls of the famous Lascaux cave in France are some 17,300 years old and demonstrate a prehistoric reverence of the natural world, perhaps even nature worship.

would be mostly generous and equable. Perhaps this was achieved by making her offerings of her bounty in propitious open air locations – by an especially venerable tree or where a camp was made for a season, for instance. Such practices would help explain why no related archaeological evidence has been preserved in the way that it has in the sheltered environment of inhabited caves. What has been found in such locations includes figurines of which the Venus of Hohle Fels is an early example. Discovered in 2008 near Schelklingen in the Swabian Alb region of Germany and between 35,000 and 40,000 years old (the Upper Palaeolithic period of Cro-Magnon man in Europe), the figurine is carved from woolly mammoth ivory and is very clearly of human female form. In the absence of a written record, interpretation of how such artefacts relate to religious concepts and ritual activities remains both hypothetical and controversial. Its discoverer, the archaeologist Nicholas J Conard interprets the figurine as 'about sex, reproduction … an extremely powerful depiction of the essence of being female'. An alternative perspective proposed by anthropologists Alan and Barnaby Dixon suggests such figurines (they have been found in several locations) represent 'hope for survival and longevity, within well-nourished and reproductively successful communities'. A third and no less valid interpretation is that early humans conceived a belief system that gave meaning to the natural processes, cycles and events that dominated and directed their lives, and that these 'well-endowed' female forms personify an earth or mother goddess whose symbolism had everything to do with fertility and nature herself.

Extrapolating forward in time the reasonable assumption that nature worship was a core component of early man's religious beliefs, it comes as no surprise to discover that such practices continued and developed in the millennia following the agricultural revolution. The richness of the archaeological record, which now includes written records, allows us to demonstrate that not only was plant reverence and nature worship intrinsic to the religions that emerged with the first civilisations but also that this worship was sophisticated and took a diversity of forms. Moreover, it reveals that by the third millennium BCE ornamental gardens imbued with a religious significance were being made. This, then, is where the global journey to reveal how and why plants and gardens are so central to religion begins.

We are bound to be selective in what we choose to look at when we study history. This book focuses on the gardens and plants of the world's belief systems. However nothing happens in isolation and this is particularly the case with the ancient civilisations, with which the book begins. Many of them were contemporaneous and developed strong connections through trade and enjoyed cultural exchanges with each other. The Cretan Minoan period (3650–1170 BCE) not only spanned the Ancient Near East Bronze Age but also paralleled Ancient Egypt from the Early Dynastic to the New Kingdom periods. At the same time but further east Mesopotamia (broadly the land mass covered by Iran and Iraq) was a far more unstable land, torn by successive dynastic wars that saw the Sumerians give way to the Akkadians followed by the subsequent rise of the Assyrians. The Minoans were followed by the Bronze Age Aegean civilisations which were in turn succeeded by Archaic Greece in about 750 BCE; a time when the Assyrians still held sway in Mesopotamia and Pharaonic Egypt was still going strong. To the west Rome was allegedly founded by Romulus and Remus in 753 BCE but her star did not begin to rise until the foundation of the Republic in 509 BCE, by which time the Achaemenid (or Persian) Empire had gained the upper hand in Mesopotamia. In 332 BCE the Macedonian Alexander the Great and his Greek army conquered Egypt from the Persians and his general Ptolemy established the Ptolemaic dynasty, but it was the Romans who conquered Greece from 146 BCE and Persia from 92 BCE, who also finally did for Ancient Egypt

in 31 BCE. Specifically at the Battle of Actium when Octavian (later Emperor Augustus) defeated the army of Mark Antony and Pharaoh Cleopatra VII.

The point of this very potted history is to show that the ancient world was not a set of isolated empires and cultures but a place where trade and conquest constantly reshaped borders. Nevertheless, with the exceptions of Roman appropriation of the Ancient Greek pantheon and some Sumerian deities subsumed into the Babylonian-Assyrian religion, each civilisation had its own, distinctive religion. None of which, with the obvious exception of Judaism which evolved throughout the first millennium BCE and which was and is practised by an ethno-religious group, is any longer active. Yet all of these religions shared – but expressed in different ways – two similarities: all held certain plants to be symbolic and all created gardens or revered sacred landscapes. The legacy and mystery of these ancient belief systems lives on in myth, legend, surviving texts, and of course the archaeological record and it is to these sources we must turn to examine and interpret the various forms of religious gardens and to identify those plants held sacred.

LEFT This Egyptian wall painting from the tomb of Nebamun dates to c.1350 BCE and the eighteenth dynasty of the New Kingdom. It shows a rectangular garden pool filled with aquatics, fish and birds surrounded by formally arranged plantings of palms and other trees.

RIGHT A detail from a fresco discovered by archaeologists in the House of Lilies at Amnisos on the island of Crete shows that the Minoan civilisation at least cultivated plants as ornamentals. The lily also had a relgio-symbolic significance.

OVERLEAF Albeit known as 'Landscape with Aeneas at Delos', this painting by Claude Lorrain (1672) suggests the importance the Romans attributed to worship in a natural setting. Such paintings also had a strong influence on the emergence of the eighteenth-century English landscape garden.

# Classical and ancient belief systems

## Egypt

The Ancient Egyptian civilisation lasted from the first until the twenty-sixth dynasty, c.3000–525 BCE when Pharaoh Psamtik III was defeated by the Persian king Cambyses II in the battle of Pelusium. Following this defeat, Egypt, together with Cyprus and Phoenicia, was subsumed within the sixth satrapy of the Achaemenid Empire. The arid, hot climate of Egypt is a boon to archaeologists as it has preserved so many artefacts that would have simply rotted away under different conditions. So, in addition to monumental architecture, statues and carved hieroglyphics, many fragile papyri, burial artefacts of wood, tomb paintings and tomb occupants, even plant materials, have survived. All of these shed considerable light on this literary and sophisticated society and, of course, on its religion and gardens.

The belief system of Ancient Egypt was polytheistic, possessed of an extensive pantheon and based on the cult of the dead. The pharaoh was both political and religious leader, deemed a living god who upon death became Osiris – brother and husband of Isis, god of the afterlife, the underworld and the dead, and therefore also of fertility, regeneration and rebirth. Thus the cult of the god was almost the same as the cult of the pharaoh and there was a strong association of vegetation and fertility with the god/pharaoh as giver and preserver of life. In death it was therefore essential that a pharaoh be remembered. The location for their cult worship was a funerary monument which was constructed during the pharaoh's lifetime and told their life story. Such monuments were also adorned with gardens and sacred plants which therefore became associated with death and the afterlife as well as fertility and renewal.

LEFT A relief in the funeral temple of Ramesses II shows the pharaoh seated before a sacred Ished tree (considered to be the persea tree). Upon the leaves of this tree of history the god Amun-Ra inscribes the pharaoh's deeds.

RIGHT The tamarisk tree was believed to be sacred to Osiris, the god of the afterlife, the underworld and the dead and therefore also of regeneration and rebirth.

One such plant was the Ished or Yshit tree which some experts consider to be the persea tree (*Mimusops laurifolia*). This was the tree of history upon whose leaves the gods depicted the name and the deeds of the pharaoh, and a lovely example of this activity is carved in the Temple of Ramesses II (r.1279–1213 BCE). Other symbolic trees included the sycomore fig (*Ficus sycomorus*) which was sacred to the goddess Hathor. Also called Nut and Isis, the sky goddess personified the principles of love, motherhood and joy, but in tombs she is depicted as mistress of the West welcoming the newly deceased into the next life and giving them sustenance.

The tamarisk tree (*Tamarix aphylla*), on the other hand, was sacred to Osiris. When his brother Set usurped and killed Osiris, the coffin came to rest under a tamarisk tree, which enclosed his body and from where he came back to life. Thus the tamarisk was seen as the tree of rebirth and of life. Given the belief that the pharaoh's soul transmigrated into Osiris, royal tombs were sometimes represented in hieroglyphic form

as the tomb of Osiris – a mound with tamarisk trees growing out of it. The mound also symbolically represented the mound of creation (the earth) and the Egyptian creation myth. The Osireion at Abydos is a realisation of this form. Built by Seti I (r. c.1290–1179 BCE), it is an integral part of his funerary complex and specifically as his memorial tomb as Osiris now that he had been transmigrated into the god. The building was covered in a mound of earth around which were dug six large tree pits in which remains of tamarisk and cypress trees were discovered. A natural spring seems to have fed a pool around the subterranean 'grave' thus representing the primeval waters from which the mound arose at the start of time.

RIGHT A detail of a twelfth-century BCE painting from the tomb of Inherkha in Deir El Medina, Thebes, showing the Ished tree which was also considered a symbol of the sun and the sun god Ra. Here Ra is seen killing the snake god Apophis.

BELOW This garden painting from the Theban tomb of army commander Amenemheb Meh and dating to the mid-eighteenth dynasty depicts a rectangular pool planted with waterlily and surrounded by a grove of formally planted trees including both the date and doum palms.

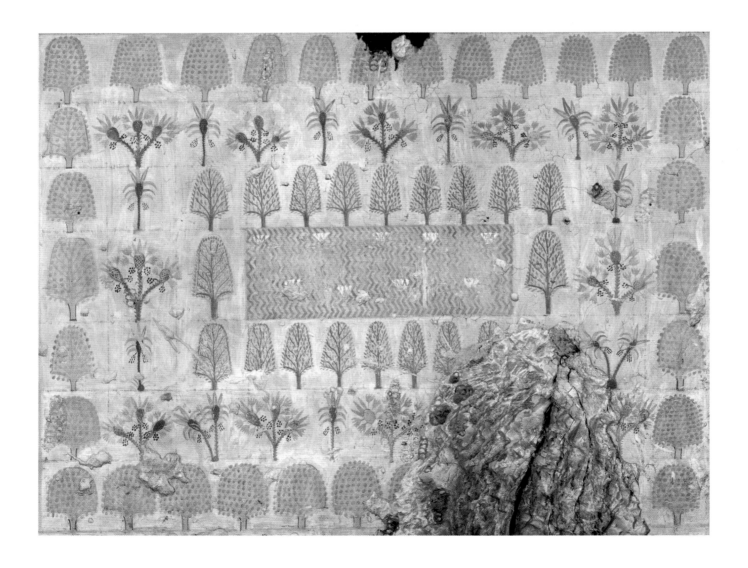

Pharaonic funerary monuments were some of the largest architectural and garden-making projects undertaken by the pharaohs. Medinet Habu is the mortuary temple precinct of Ramesses III ( r.1186–1155 BCE) on the west bank of the Nile at Luxor and measures an impressive 210 by 230 metres (230 by 251 yards) with the temple itself some 150 metres (164 yards) long. Ramesses himself wrote that the vast funerary temple was surrounded with gardens and groves filled with fruit trees and flowers 'for the two serpent goddesses'. Here too were lakes in which grew lotus (the blue waterlily, *Nymphaea caerulea*) and among the temple buildings were gardens 'planted with trees and vegetation like the [Nile] Delta'. Older still is Djeser-Djeseru, the main building of the funerary temple complex constructed by Pharoah Hatshepsut (r. c.1475–1458 BCE).

For those other than the pharaoh living was a preparation for the desired afterlife, Aaru or the Field of Reeds. A destination the departed soul reached having first navigated (with

ABOVE A mature sycamore fig tree is a splendid sight. It is also the columnar tree surrounding the pool in the garden tomb painting opposite. The tree was sacred to the goddess Hathor whose avatars included Nut and Isis.

the aid of *The Book of the Dead*) the perilous journey of the underworld and the weighing-of-the-soul trial in the Hall of Judgement. Aaru was a facsimile of the munificent Nile valley but better. A version without disease or hunger, where the climate was always gentle, where humans coexisted harmoniously with abundant animals, where plants grew ebulliently and no labour was required to care for either. This set of ideal attributes was also met by both the ancient Greek Elysium and Isles of the Blessed and the afterlife realms that appear in Celtic, Islamic and Pure Land Buddhist belief systems. Moreover the same attributes are emphasised in Dilmun, the Sumerian garden of the gods, and were enjoyed on earth during those times of mankind's innocence, namely the Greek Golden Age and the Judaeo-Christian Eden.

# Pharaoh Hatshepsut's funerary monument
## Deir el Bahari, Egypt

Djeser-Djeseru was designed by architect Senenmout and is located on the west bank of the Nile and aligned onto the Temple of Amun (a local Theban god) on the opposite bank at Karnak. Rising in terraces Hatshepsut's temple merges into the sheer limestone cliffs of Deir el Bahari in which it was believed Hathor resided. From the river and leading up to the second terrace was an avenue lined with 120 huge statues at 10 metre spacings. Depicting the queen as a sphinx, they represented the power of Egypt and acted as guardians of the approach, which was also lined from the river to the outer court with an avenue of trees. Either side of the gateway leading into this court the tree pits dug into the rock were found to contain remains of the persea tree.

In the middle of the outer court and on either side of the path leading to the ramp that ascends to the first terrace was a T-shaped pool. Water was of particular significance to a cult temple as it was believed that here the pharaoh/god could refresh herself, while the pool itself would have been a site where offerings were made to the dead queen.

The pool was planted with papyrus which was believed to be another home of Hathor and in a temple setting was used in both its dedication and during funerary rites. Around the pools about 66 pits were cut into the rock and probably planted with trees to form a shady grove.

On the second and third terrace Hatshepsut appears in statue form as Osiris. Within the innermost shrine on the upper terrace are two wall carvings showing a fish pool planted with lotus beside which are gardens devoted to growing bitter lettuce (*Lactuca serriola*), a perceived aphrodisiac and sacred to the phallic creation divinity Amun-Min. Here too is depicted the first record of plant hunting. In 1493 BCE Hatshepsut sent an expedition to Punt (no one knows where this was but best guess is on the western coast of the Red Sea, somewhere in present-day Somalia, the Sudan or Eritrea) to collect trees of frankincense (*Boswellia frereana*) and myrrh (*Commiphora erythraea*). It is possible that these rarities were grown at Djeser-Djeseru, perhaps in pots or in the tree pits.

The face of pharaoh Hatshepsut, arguably the most accomplished queen of Ancient Egypt.

OPPOSITE Hatshepsut's funerary monument in the Valley of the Queens merges into the sheer limestone cliffs of Deir el Bahari which, it was believed, were inhabited by Hathor.

LEFT A relief in the uppermost temple depicts soldiers carrying incense trees in baskets — the bounty from the first recorded plant-hunting expedition, ordered by Hatshepsut.

OVERLEAF Now surrounded by arid sand and rock, the approach to and courtyards of this striking monument would once have been green with plants that had a symbolic association with the pharaoh.

One of the delights to be enjoyed in Aaru was a garden, and just as life was a preparation for the afterlife, so the gardens made along the Nile valley were of a form of which an even better, improved version was hoped for in Aaru. Archaeologists have uncovered physical remains of gardens but the most comprehensive and detailed evidence for both constructed and anticipated gardens is in the form of grave goods (model gardens and depictions on papyri) and tomb paintings. The most famous and most detailed example of the latter belonged to Sennufer, Mayor of Thebes and chief gardener to Amenophis II (r. c.1427–1401 BCE). Painted on the wall of Tomb 96 at Thebes this is the oldest known depiction of an ornamental garden but its design reveals that

RIGHT AND BELOW Papyrus was not only made into a form of paper it was also believed to be another home of Hathor and thus had funerary associations.

by this date garden art had already evolved to a relatively sophisticated level. Interestingly, archaeological evidence from subsequent dynasties reveals that the Ancient Egyptian garden style did not change markedly from this time on.

The representation, however, is not of Sennufer's own garden – although it may be indicative of what he was hoping for in Aaru. One of his titles was 'Overseer of the Gardens of Amun' and the painting is thought to depict one of the gardens of the Temple of Amun at Karnak. Temples were believed to be inhabited by the gods and thus to represent the universe, the land of Egypt and an earthly expression of heaven. Their gardens too were believed to be sacred and inhabited by the gods themselves, and so played an integral role in cult temples activities. In addition they symbolised growth, harvest and renewal and gave reality to mythological places described in religious texts.

In this specific example, possibly the garden located west of the Third Pylon and beside the western approach to the temple, the style is ornamental and of a form that developed in response to climate and location. The impression is very much of an escape from a harsh desert into a refreshing, verdant, shady, cool and well-watered haven. The square plot was enclosed behind high walls to keep out the hot, drying

ABOVE The strikingly beautiful blue waterlily was, for obvious reasons, a plant associated with the sun god Ra. It has recently been discovered to have narcotic properties and is probably the lotus of the Ancient world.

BELOW In this vignette from a copy of *The Book of the Dead* belonging to Nakhte, the deceased scribe and his wife stand in a formal garden. Painted on papyrus this may depict the garden the couple hoped for in the afterlife of Aaru.

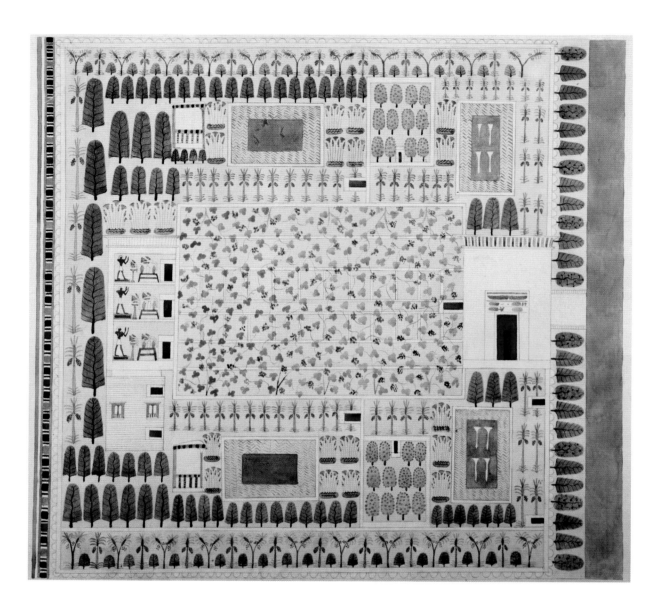

and sand-laden winds (as well as animal and human intruders). A canal or lake is shown adjacent to the walls with the large pylonic gateway approached by an avenue of trees leading from a landing stage that was itself reached from the water. Facing the imposing gateway on the far side of the quad is the shrine to Amun, divided into three areas and containing statues of the god as well as offerings made to him. The position of the shrine in relation to the gateway generates a main axis around which the formally designed garden is symmetrical. In the centre is a large, rectangular vine-clad pergola on either side of which are a pavilion or kiosk and a pair of grass-edged, rectangular pools perpendicular to one another. Water represented the original water which covered the earth at the beginning of time (from which the Mound arose) and was the god called Nun. The planting made full use of the Nile valley's rich alluvial soil and irrigation by the river's waters. Beside

the pools were papyrus and floating in it was lotus. With its flowers that sink beneath the water every night to rise and open again in the morning, and with its striking sky-blue petals and sun-yellow anthers it is no surprise that this aquatic was a sign of rebirth and sacred to the sun god Ra who was believed to rule in all parts of the created world: the sky, the earth and the underworld, and who, new born every morning, emerged as the sun god rising out of a floating lotus. Other plants associated with water and depicted on a wooden box showing Tutankhamun (r. *c*.1332–1323 BCE) hunting fish with a bow and arrow are mandrake (*Mandragora officinarum*), poppy (*Papaver rhoeas*) and a form of knapweed (*Cyanus depressus*).

A network of straight paths pass beneath avenues of a single tree type (although underplanted in one case), all of which had a sacro-religious significance: the tamarisk and sycomore fig, the date palm (*Phoenix dactylifera*) sacred to

ABOVE A pavement fragment painted with a lotus from the palace of Akhenaten, c.1353–1336 BCE

LEFT This watercolour copy depicts the famous garden painted on a wall of the tomb of Sennufer discovered in the Tombs of the Nobles, Thebes. Already by the late fifteenth century BCE Egyptian garden design had reached a high level of sophistication and was charged with religious symbolism.

RIGHT A limestone stele from the royal tomb at Amarna showing Akhenaten offering lotus flowers to the sun god Aten.

providing some of the thirty-one plant products recorded as used during mummification. According to the Greek historian Herodotus, after desiccation the body was treated with myrrh, cassia and 'every sort of spicery except frankincense'. Certain plants were placed on the body, for example small onions were found in the eye sockets of Ramesses IV, while the body was wound with linen wrappings and placed in a coffin made variously of cedar, sycomore fig and oak.

And just as temple gardens were inhabited by the gods so too did palace gardens have a religious symbolism as sites of cult activity of the pharaoh/god. As such they were similarly laid out and enhanced with displays of symbolic sculpture and statuary showing the garden owner in various guises and occupations and emphasising his/her relationship with the gods. Examples of this form of garden were made by Akhenaten (r. c.1353–1336 BCE) in his garden city of Amarna.

Ra and the branching doum palm (*Hyphaene thebaica*) sacred to Thoth. Often considered to be the heart (believed then to be the repository of the mind), Thoth was also considered to be the tongue of Ra, the means by which Ra's will was translated into speech. Taken together the planting offered beauty, shade, ornament and fruits as well as some of the produce required for temple offerings. Indeed, one of Sennufer's temple duties was to present the 'scent of the marshes' flowers, and all kinds of plants from amongst the finest of the orchard which his Majesty has made anew for his Father Amun Ra, . . . on behalf of his Majesty'. Additional offerings (flowers were also processed into perfumes, unguents and garlands) would have been provided by temple-owned flower gardens, orchards and groves located away from the temple itself. Such gardens would also have generated an income from sales of fruit and wood for building or fuel as well as

# Minoan

The Minoan civilisation of Crete was the first Mediterranean thalassocracy. Theirs was an advanced culture whose palaces were built without defensive walls and whose wealth came from maritime trade. But much of Minoan civilisation remains a mystery. Who knows what the clay tablets inscribed with Linear A may tell us about Minoan life and culture, religious practices and gardens? But until such time as the language is deciphered it is to the physical archaeological record we must turn for such facts as can be established. Even so, there are only so many definites that artefacts and sites can tell us in the absence of a confirmatory narrative; much of the interpretation must remain hypothetical. For example, the beautifully painted Haghia Triada sarcophagus (1370–1320 BCE) found at a villa site near the palace of Phaistos on the south coast has been interpreted as depicting religious rites in connection with the dead and the soul's journey to the afterlife and some authorities claim these have an Egyptian influence. However, none of this can be substantiated and in many ways the artworks ask more questions than they answer. Indeed there are relatively few specifics known about the Minoan belief system beyond the fact that it was a matriarchal goddess religion. Exactly who inhabited its pantheon and what if any were its creation myths and afterlife beliefs we do not know.

Did the Minoans make gardens? Again the simple answer is we don't know. But a 1.8 metre (2 yard) tall frieze found in the House of the Lilies at Amnisos to the east of Heraklion on the north coast and dating to c.1550–1500 BCE shows papyrus, *Iris* spp., *Mentha* spp. and lilies in red, blue and white growing in pots. Papyrus is not native to Crete and its presence demonstrates Minoan links with Ancient Egypt. Whilst the scene is not necessarily an ornamental garden the fresco does reveal that Minoans imported and cultivated plants outside their natural habitat to be enjoyed ornamentally. There is little other evidence to indicate that the Minoans made garden art forms whether ornamental and/or sacro-religious in the way the Egyptians did. Thus the first conclusion must be that while the Minoans lived amidst a naturally beautiful,

BELOW Discovered at Haghia Triada and dating to the fourteenth century BCE, this beautifully made and decorated Minoan sarcophagus may … or may not … depict a death cult scene.

RIGHT The natural beauty of the Cretan landscape and its diverse and equally lovely flora may have inspired nature worship among the Minoans. Here poppy anemones grow among candia tulips on the Omalos plateau in the White Mountains.

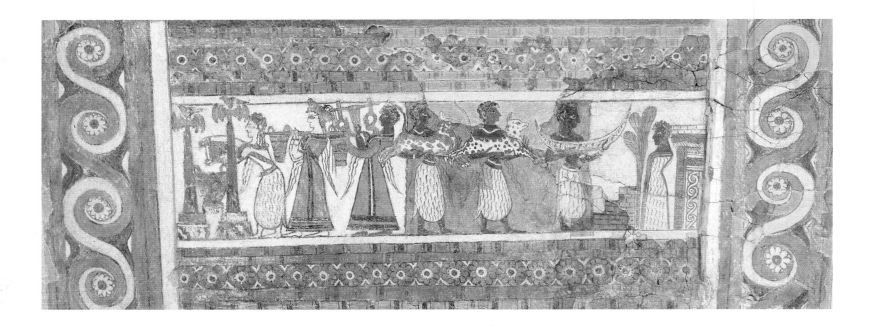

well-watered and floriferous landscape blessed by a generous climate, they (together with mainland Ancient Greeks – as we shall discover) were the least garden-centric civilisation of the ancient world.

Peak sanctuaries such as that on the top of Mount Juktas, hilltop shrines and sacred cave sites do however reveal that the Minoans conducted ritual and ceremony within natural settings (peak sanctuaries and hilltop shrines had buildings so the religious activity was not necessarily al fresco) and highly revered the natural world, or more accurately the spirit of nature, be it wild or tamed. This assumption about the practice of religious activities within a natural setting is supported by the fact that no palatial archaeological site has revealed separate buildings identifiable as temples, although rooms within palace complexes are thought to have been used for religious practice.

The finest depiction of a peak sanctuary is the relief carving that decorates the Sanctuary Rhyton, a graceful chlorite vessel standing about 30 centimetres (12 inches) tall which was discovered at the palace of Zakros on the eastern coast of Crete. The relief depicts a tripartite shrine adorned with horns of consecration and crowned, perhaps symbolically, with two birds and four agrimis (wild, long-horned goats native to Crete). The shrine is set within a rocky wilderness in which two further agrimis scamper and flowers, including crocus, grow. Other nature-centric artefacts including glyptic art in the form of seals and rings, frescoes and votive offerings further indicate a sacred or religious narrative centred on nature in which certain plants and landscapes were imbued with strong, symbolic meaning.

The Ring of Minos (c.1500 BCE) is one of a number of golden rings engraved with representations of cult activity conducted in a natural setting. The main scene may be a seashore cult event but it clearly has an arboreal aspect to it. Two female figures pay reverence to two trees, one of which surmounts a hilltop shrine or peak sanctuary. Their attitude also suggests that they are bending the branches towards the goddess seated by a shrine and near a set of sacral horns. Could this be in veneration of her as a tree divinity or nature goddess, or are they shaking the sacred trees in order to attract her attention as a fructifying goddess of harvest or fertility?

Of a similar age and also discovered on Crete the Isopata Ring (1600–1400 BCE) shows four women performing an ecstatic ritual dance of benediction in a meadow dotted with lilies. Is this dance associated with a nature goddess or an epiphany of the spring goddess (a precursor of Chloris)? Once again, we cannot be sure. And another, fifteenth-century BCE gold signet ring from the Acropolis treasure at Mycenae on mainland Greece similarly depicts what could be an epiphany scene with two women/priestesses and a female child clad in Minoan garb and with that most Minoan of motifs, the labrys or symmetric double-headed axe. The scene provides evidence that flowers were harvested and used in rituals for the two women are offering flowers – possibly lilies and the sea

ABOVE One of several clay figurines found in a shrine at Gazi near Heraklion that have headdresses of opium poppy seed capsules and which may represent a poppy goddess.

Three oval golden rings depicting nature cult activities. The Ring of Minos shows a scene of nature worship possibly involving trees and the seashore.

The Isopata Ring from Knossos shows women dancing ecstatically in a flower-filled meadow.

From Tomb V Circle A at Mycenae this ring may depict an epiphany scene involving the poppy goddess.

daffodil (*Pancratium maritimum*) to a goddess figure seated beneath a tree shrine or more likely a specimen of the now extinct but very tall silphion. This lost plant is thought to have been a member of the genus *Ferula* and resembled *F. asa-foetida*. It was indigenous only to the Cyrenaica peninsula in eastern Libya and was in antiquity considered a universal remedy and an aphrodisiac. The fact that the goddess, seated beneath this stimulating plant, is also holding three seed capsules of the opium poppy (*Papaver somniferum*), a plant whose latex produces euphoria, suggests that she may be a Minoan representation of the goddess of love. Alternatively she could be the poppy goddess, revered as a bringer of joy and intoxication, the existence of whom is supported by five

RIGHT The beautiful sea daffodil grows on Cretan sand dunes just above the high tide line where its large drifts create a natural and very ethereal spectacle.

BELOW This detail from the fresco painted above a lustral basin in Xeste 3 on the island of Thera (Santorini) shows two young women harvesting saffron in a natural landscape.

clay figurines discovered at a sanctuary site at Gazi to the west of Heraklion. Each idol has her arms raised and eyes closed and wears a headdress adorned with opium poppy capsules. Delightfully, and in spite the simplicity of the form, the largest figurine appears to be smiling, perhaps in a state of euphoria. Also found at the excavation site was a tubular vase with a base and a hole on the sides, assumed to be used for preparing inhalations of opium.

A third option is that the seated goddess is of one of healing – opium being revered as a bringer of pain relief in a therapeutic context and associated with the perceived curative properties of silphion.

A number of frescoes discovered in palaces, villas and houses also reveal that plants had a strong sacro-religious role in Minoan life. The Prince of the Lilies fresco from the palace of Knossos just south of Heraklion depicts a royal or religious figure wearing a necklace of lilies and a crown of lilies and peacock feathers (the restored background of a field of lilies is not based on archaeological evidence). Found in the villa at Haghia Triadha and dating to c.1600–1450 BCE another scene depicts a kneeling woman in a florally-rich landscape setting. Despite the presence of a goddess such a form of genuflection was unknown in Aegean cultures and thus she is not worshipping. Rather she is ritualistically gathering the stigma of the native saffron crocus (*Crocus cartwrightianus*). A similar harvest is depicted in the Crocus Gatherer from the palace at Knossos which shows crocus growing in a rocky landscape, identifiable as such by the undulations. In another fresco from Knossos a monkey is shown amidst papyrus. This suggests the scene may be a sacred landscape for neither the animals nor plants are native to Crete and must be either imported or mythological. The religio-symbolism of the monkey is underlined by a scene from Xeste 3, part of the excavation of the Minoan settlement at Akrotiri on the island of Thera (Santorini) which was, Pompeii-like, buried and wonderfully preserved in volcanic ash by the c.1627 BCE eruption of the island. Painted over two adjacent walls is a

LEFT The restored fresco of the Prince of the Lilies which was discovered in the palace of Knossos in Crete. Note his crown and necklace of lily blooms.

BELOW The striking, red flowering *Lilium chalcedonicum* is one of a number of Cretan native plants that played a significant if unknown role in Minoan religion.

rocky landscape in which a monkey acts as the intermediary (or perhaps emblem of the goddess) presenting the stigmas harvested by the women/priestesses to the goddess who sits on a raised stool beside a griffin.

Certainly saffron was revered, for as well as the depictions of it as an offering, the famous figurine of the serpent goddess is clad in a dress dyed a saffron yellow. Another fresco from Thera depicts a woman applying saffron to treat her bleeding foot, indicating a medicinal use, and no doubt it was also used as a spice. But who was this 'saffron goddess'? Perhaps she was a nature goddess, and associated with healing and fertility. A tenuous link for the latter can be made between the serpent goddess in her saffron-dyed dress and Sumerian belief systems in which the snake had a fertility symbolism.

Although not native to the Greek islands, monkeys were intimately associated with plant reverence in Minoan religion and may have been a familiar of a nature goddess. In this detail of the Blue Monkey fresco from the palace of Knossos (left) monkeys are gathering papyrus and on the fresco discovered in the Room of the Blue Monkeys at Akrotiri, Thera (below) a troop of monkeys pluck a harvest of saffron in a rocky landscape.

RIGHT Dating to c.1600 BCE and discovered in the palace of Knossos the dress of this famous statue of the younger snake goddess is dyed a saffron yellow colour.

Or, as with the anthers of the lotus in Egypt, perhaps the yellow of the saffron had an association with the sun.

One notable difference between the landscape frescoes found on Thera and those on Crete is that the former are more representational and lifelike and the latter more exotic and fantastical. This is clear when a comparison is made between the Theran scene of crocus-gathering and another rocky but more floriferous landscape from the House of the Frescoes at Knossos, a scene of birds and monkeys (indicating the presence of the nature goddess?) within a seemingly wild landscape. The relatively high number of frescoes depicting plants, specifically ivy (*Hedera* spp.), papyrus, roses, sea daffodil, Madonna lily (*Lilium candidum*) and *L. chalcedonicum*, and of course crocus, displayed within a stylised naturalistic landscape as against other subjects, suggests that the plants themselves were also of equal sacro-religious significance.

Nature is depicted as both wild and tamed and while the former was probably revered the latter strongly suggests that the Minoans cultivated nature sanctuaries – locations within an already beautiful, wild nature which were imbued with an especial significance and where nature was gently and subtly tended in order to create sacred groves or meadows. They would have been liminal places between the human and supernatural world that also supplied vegetative offerings. Such a cultivated, sacred and adored nature is perhaps the setting for the aforementioned kneeling saffron-gatherer in the Haghia Triadha fresco. The full scene covers three walls in one flowing and flowering triptych. The undulations once again indicate this is a rocky landscape. On the left-hand wall, even though enlivened with native lilies and crocus, the landscape appears to be tamed, serene and humanised. The contrasting scene on the right-hand wall is animated (literally) with a population of birds and beasts set amongst a riot of plants, a wilder 'true' nature. It is not a huge leap of imagination to envisage that the lady in the left-hand scene is a priestess tending a nature sanctuary and gathering crocus stigma to offer to the nature goddess who occupies the middle wall in a position that artistically and symbolically bridges the two domains. Perhaps too these sacred landscapes set

within nature inspired what might just be an example of a Minoan garden. In the south-eastern corner of the palace of Phaistos and located at the terminus of a court commanding a view out over the borrowed landscape of the steep valley beyond is a naturally-occurring, picturesque rocky outcrop. Into this outcrop have been cut a series of holes that are the perfect size to receive flower bulbs or plants. When in bloom these would have created a miniaturised and stylised nature sanctuary-cum-garden. A living, three-dimensional example of what was painted inside and on so many walls.

# Mesopotamia

Ancient Mesopotamia has a timeline that is contiguous with Ancient Egypt but its regional history is far more complex being riven with wars and a succession of empires whose geographical extents varied: the Sumerians (c.5000–2400 BCE), the Akkadians (2334–2154 BCE), the Assyrians (c.2000–400 BCE), the Babylonians and Medes (612–539 BCE) and finally the Achaemenians or Persians (539–330 BCE). Nevertheless one constant in Mesopotamia, aside from war, was a reverence for plants and a delight in garden-making.

Unlike the Egyptians with their fantastically formed deities, the Sumerians believed that the universe was administered by a pantheon of living beings similar in form to humans but superior to them in nature and power.

Deities included those associated with the sun, moon and other celestial objects, the earth, water, underworld, cities, even mundane objects such as pickaxes, brick moulds and ploughs. And in the absence of a Minoan narrative it appears that the notion of a divine paradise garden as the home of the immortals is of Sumerian origin. Named Dilmun it is described in the Sumerian myth of Enki and Ninhursaga and according to Dina Katz the text describes Dilmun as pure, pristine and virginal. A place where animals lived in harmony with one another, there was no sickness or ageing or disrespect, no crime and to which Enki brings 'sweet water'. Here too the sexually promiscuous Enki not only impregnated Ninhursaga, the earth mother, most exalted lady and supreme queen, but also their subsequent offspring, until Ninhursaga advises her

great-granddaughter Uttu to reject Enki unless he brings her a gift of fruit. He does so and she receives him but uses his semen to produce eight different plants. These Enki eats, infuriating Ninhursaga who curses him. Enki begins to die and in the end Ninhursaga relents and revives him. Other Sumerian texts describe Dilmun as located at 'the place where the sun rises', that is to say to the east and there are a number of clear parallels between Sumerian and biblical motifs including an earthly garden paradise ('planted eastward in Eden') and the consumption of sacred plants with deleterious effect. However, it must be remembered that chronology prevents the Sumerians from having directly influenced later Hebrew writers, and the biblical stories probably descended via the Canaanites.

The Sumerians also gave us one of the earliest surviving works of literature, *The Epic of Gilgamesh*. The single volume 'Old Babylonian' version written in Akkadian and dating to the eighteenth century BCE is a compilation of five independent Sumerian poems dating to as early as the Third Dynasty of Ur (2150–2000 BCE). Our eponymous hero is the demi-god king of the city of Uruk: 'One third of the whole is city, one third is garden, and one third is field, with the precinct of the goddess Inanna'. Inanna was goddess of fertility, love, war and sex and the counterpart of the Akkadian, Assyrian and Babylonian Ishtar. More information about her temple precinct is given in a separate myth-poem 'Inanna and the Huluppu Tree' (part of the Gilgamesh, Enkidu and the Netherworld tale). Desirous to make a throne and marriage bed from its timber Inanna nurtures a huluppu tree (possibly a willow or a date palm) within her sacred sanctuary garden. As it matures the huluppu tree acquires a bird in its branches and a snake among its roots, and once the tree reaches sufficient girth Gilgamesh enters the garden, evicts the bird, kills the serpent and fells the tree. There is much symbolism tied up in this tale but a dominant theme is fertility. The fertility goddess with her 'fruitful garden', a snake which was often connected with the same subject and in androcentric Mesopotamia the king usually held the title 'Gardener'. Indeed, gardening and ploughing could be metaphors for taking the male part in sexual intercourse. For example, in one Sumerian love poem Inanna sings of her

vulva, her 'uncultivated land', and asks, 'Who will plough it?' Metaphorically, then, the fertile grove is the goddess but in the huluppu poem the garden was 'fruitful' in and of itself.

Another concept introduced in the huluppu myth is that of a world tree. The huluppu is symbolically the *axis mundi* (world axis), a motif present in several religions and mythologies of both Indo-European and American origin. The world tree is represented as a colossal tree which supports the sky, thereby connecting the heavens, the world and through its roots the underworld. It may also be strongly connected to the motif of the tree of life. In Babylonia the tree of life was called the tree of Ea, the father of the gods and those who ate its fruit were supposed to receive eternal life. It grew in Eridu (present day Abu Shahrein) which was considered the first city in the world by the Sumerians and sometimes named as a location of the Sumerian paradise. And, of course, immortality-giving fruit features in Genesis 3:22 ('And the Lord God said, Behold, the man is become as one of us, to know good and evil: and now, lest he put forth his hand, and take also of the tree of life, and eat, and live for ever'), the Greek myth of the Garden of the Hesperides and Viking legend.

It was also a snake in the *Epic* which stole from Gilgamesh while he bathed the prickly plant which he had gathered from the bottom of the sea and which he had been promised would restore his youthfulness. This secret had been imparted by his immortal ancestor Utanapishtim the Noah-like figure at

LEFT In this Neo-Assyrian scene a lady, holding a mace, worships the armed goddess Ishtar in her aspect as goddess of war. Other symbols including the palm tree and the goats point to Ishtar's fertility aspect.

ABOVE In the ancient world the cedar of Lebanon was both revered and much prized for its timber, which has sadly resulted in its near extinction in its native habitat.

the centre of the Sumerian flood myth (which took place in Dilmun) and 'whom the gods took after the deluge' and from whom Gilgamesh desired to learn the secret of eternal life. Gilgamesh's perilous journey to find Utanapishtim was undertaken following the death of his friend and companion Enkidu which had resulted from the pair defeating and killing Humbaba, the guardian monster of the sacred cedar forest. This sacred forest of cedar of Lebanon (*Cedrus libani*) was a home to the gods and the pair had desecrated it by felling the unique tree. The vast wilderness of the forest, its deep gloom beneath the canopy and its thick luxuriant growth suggest an otherworldliness of nature. This is in stark contrast to the next realm of the gods that Gilgamesh enters having endured the trial of darkness. The brilliant 'garden of the gods' was a magical realm, a preternaturally immaculate garden of trees made of precious stones which bear jewelled fruits, a wondrous orchard set between high mountains that reach to the sky and the encircling sea which is reminiscent of the Greek myth of the Garden of the Hesperides (see p.48). The third and last paradise garden reached by Gilgamesh is Dilmun wherein dwelt Utanapishtim.

Sumerian deities were adopted into the Babylonian-Assyrian pantheon and the use of temple gardens as locations for cult ceremonies is attested to during Assyrian times. Enil, god of the air, for example, had a pleasant temple garden which bore rich fruits, where the birds brooded and giant carp played. And as part of the New Year festival in the city of Ashur a statue of Anu, the god of heaven, lord of constellations, king of gods, spirits and demons was carried in procession from his temple within the city through the Akitu temple garden which was located outside the city and was possibly contiguous with the royal garden. The latter was described by King

ABOVE Dating to the mid-ninth century BCE this relief depicts king Ashurnasirpal II and the god Ashur standing beside an object that archaeologists and scholars generically term the Assyrian Sacred Tree.

BELOW A plate from *Monument de Ninive* showing Sargon II's garden in Dur-Sharrukin. Rising above the lake and its pavilion is a man-made hill crowned with a shrine and formally planted with groves of trees. Fruit trees are also present.

RIGHT The stone relief from the palace of Ashurbanipal at Nineveh shows a similar royal garden complex, but here an aqueduct feeds rills that flow down the hillside.

Sennacherib (r.705–681 BCE) as 'luxurious with sasa-fruit orchards'. Within the city archaeologists have uncovered the Temple of Ashur and surrounding it found evidence for the sole known example of a temple grove. Tree pits reveal rows of trees planted in a formal arrangement with a second plantation within the temple's central courtyard.

Thus from Sumerian times onward, and as in Egypt, the gods were believed to inhabit both temples and their associated gardens, but unfortunately we have neither the comparative descriptions nor sufficient on-the-ground archaeological evidence from which to ascertain their form. This is in large part because cities and temples together with their sacred groves were often sacked and destroyed in the course of this region's volatile history but also because the materials used, for example mud bricks, have not preserved well in the archaeological record. An exception, however, are the stone-carved and evocative bas-relief panels that adorned many royal palaces. These depict both royal gardens and a form of Assyrian tree veneration. To deal with the latter first: The city of Nimrud (Calah) was rebuilt by Ashurnasirpal II (r.883–859 BCE) who planted orchards 'with all kinds of fruit trees and vines' round about the city. Discovered in the North West Palace are reliefs that frequently depict an object that is generally referred to by scholars as the Assyrian Sacred Tree.

There is, of course, academic debate about exactly what the object is: a stylised palm tree, a cult object, an emblem of vegetation or 'tree of life', an imperial or divine symbol, or a combination of these forms? Assuming that what is depicted was modelled on a physical form, the object is composed of a tree trunk set upon a base and surmounted by a plant motif that consists of seven large fronds arranged into a palmette. The trunk is generally divided into three tiers of varying heights and widths with the sections joined by a form of ornamental C-shaped brace. Surface decoration consists of chevroned lines on the tree trunk and on the fronds of the palmette (possibly a cross-section of a rosette). Framing the trunk is a garland of palmate flowers connected to the trunk and one another by a ribbon-like stem. A possible explanation is that the trunk and crowning palmette symbolically represent the date palm tree, which was associated with Innana/Ishtar and thus fertility. If this is so then the eagle-headed gods and priests of the king often depicted as attending the object with pinecones and holding buckets could be performing a pollination fertility rite and/or receiving power from the tree. Furthermore, the object may allegorically represent the monarch's perceived fertility role as 'Gardener', and more significantly the divine world order in which the king himself represented the realisation of that order in man. In other

words the king as a true image of God represented the Perfect Man. Once again this is all speculation for surprisingly, given the frequency of its depiction, there is no written source describing the mythical-symbolic motif.

A logical extension of the king's symbolic role as gardener was for him to make gardens. King Sargon II (r.722–705 BCE) built his new city of Dur-Sharrukin (the ruins lie at Khorsabad some 20 kilometres (12 miles) north of Nineveh) and around his palace he made a large ornamental garden. A relief, illustrated in the second volume of the misnamed *Monument de Ninive* (1849), shows a pillared pavilion beside a lake, orchards and meadows and formally planted groves of coniferous trees covering an artificial mount surmounted with a shrine. This landscape was made 'like the Amanus mountains, wherein all flowers from the Hittite land and herbs from the hill are planted together' with 'the fruit trees of every mountain' and surviving correspondence mentions the moving of thousands of young fruit trees, quinces, almonds, apples and medlars to the garden. In turn Sargon's son, Sennacherib, moved his capital to Nineveh where he claims to have created 'a great park like unto Mount Amanus', and dating to the reign of Sennacherib's grandson, Ashurbanipal (r.668–c.627 BCE), the bas-reliefs in the small Room H of the North Palace at Nineveh show another royal garden complex with a grove-covered mound this time surmounted with a pavilion and well irrigated with streams fed by an aqueduct tumbling down the hillside.

The Amanus mountain range (now the Nur Mountains) reach a maximum elevation of 2240 metres (2450 yards) and is located in south-central Turkey where it divides the coastal region of Cilicia from inland Syria. Thus on the flat marshes of Babylonia the intent of successive Assyrian kings was to imitate natural, mountainous and diverse landscapes that were much about the cult of the king. Created by monarchs able to order and finance their construction and have plants sent from distant corners of the empire by loyal satraps to fill them, these royal gardens were displays of power-gardening with attendant kingly associations of power and triumphant victory. Yet they were also symbolic of peaceful pleasure, munificence and fertility and were locations for rites and ceremony observing the sovereign's religious capacity as the Perfect Man and deliverer of divine fertility.

The most famous garden made in Mesopotamia was the Hanging Gardens of Babylon. The name still evokes a sense of exotic romance for the garden was supposedly made as a love token by the Neo-Babylonian king Nebuchadnezzar II (r.605–562 BCE) around 600 BCE in order to cheer up his homesick wife Amytis of Media who longed for the trees, fragrant plants and topography of her homeland. But exactly where, even if, the cascading garden was constructed is something that generates heated debate. However, the Assyrian tradition of making designed, botanically rich landscapes was continued by the Achaemenid Empire, founded by Cyrus the Great (r. 559–530). The new form of Achaemenid garden gave

ABOVE A somewhat stylised engraving from 1845 showing the ruins of the temple of Cybele at Sardis. Near to here Cyrus made an extensive *pairidaēza* which he personally planted.

LEFT The ruins of Pasargadae. Built by the Persian king Cyrus the Great the palace was once surrounded by ornate gardens while his tomb was set within a *pairidaēza*.

rise to a new garden term. There is much academic discussion around its etymology but in essence the word *pairidaēza*, from the Median *pair* (around) and *daēza* (wall) and basically meaning an enclosed garden, gives us the Greek *paradeisos* and hence 'paradise'. A botanical *pairidaēza* (as opposed to a hunting *pairidaēza* which was basically an area of enclosed, game-stocked natural landscape) was walled about, well-watered and planted with meadows, flowers and collections of ornamental and fruit trees – often formally planted in groves. Within the grounds were also buildings such as pavilions, shrines, and occasionally tombs. The Greek soldier and historian Xenophon gives a description of Cyrus's *pairidaēza* at Sardis in Book IV of his Socratic dialogue *Oeconomicus*. The Greek Lysander went to Cyrus:

> who entertained him, and amongst other marks of courtesy showed him his 'paradise' at Sardis. Lysander was astonished at the beauty of the trees within, all planted at equal intervals, the long straight rows of waving branches, the perfect regularity, the rectangular symmetry of the whole, and the many sweet scents which hung about them as they paced the park. In

admiration he exclaimed to Cyrus: 'All this beauty is marvellous enough, but what astonishes me still more is the talent of the artificer who mapped out and arranged for you the several parts of this fair scene.' Cyrus was pleased by the remark, and said: 'Know then, Lysander, it is I who measured and arranged it all. Some of the trees', he added, 'I planted with my own hands.'

Certainly *pairidaēza* had a symbolic function as the location of associated cult activities. There was a continuation of celebrating the king's role in the provision of fecund fertility and young boys of noble birth were taught to cultivate and revere trees. Certainly the magi who tended the tomb of Cyrus built within the *pairidaēza* at Pasargadae (which Alexander the Great saw in 330 BCE and recorded that it stood in an irrigated grove of trees) carried out religious rituals. Arrian (*Anabasis* 6.29) speaks of a monthly horse sacrifice. *Pairidaēza* additionally provided plant material for festivals and ceremonies but the surviving literature gives no impression of *pairidaēza* as revered places which might have prompted intimations of the divine that was such a feature of ancient Greek religion.

Cyrus's most religio-significant garden was that made between the two palaces at Pasargadae (from 546 BCE) and contained the earliest known example of the Persian quadripartite or fourfold garden design in which straight water channels carved out of limestone blocks divided the garden space into four quarters or beds. These would probably have been planted with a mix of trees – cypress, pomegranate and cherry, and flowers such as roses, lilies and jasmine. This quadripartite form is thought to have symbolised the Achaemenid universe divided by four rivers. Nevertheless the idea of four streams flowing from a divine source to water the four corners of the earth is represented graphically in a couple of much earlier finds. An eighteenth-century BCE investiture fresco found in the palace of Zimri-Lim at Mari in eastern Syria shows the goddess Lama dispensing water from a round vase out of which grow flowers and flow four fish-filled streams going out in different directions. Similarly, an ivory inlay from thirteenth-century Ashur features a centrally positioned god from whom four streams flow.

The significance of four rivers within a paradise garden will be examined further in the next chapter when we discuss the Judaeo-Christian Eden creation myth and jannah, the Islamic after-life paradise.

# Greece

If the religious history of Mesopotamia and in particular the Achaemenid Empire is somewhat clouded, it can be said for certain that garden-making was intrinsic to the successive civilisations that ruled this land. The opposite is true of Ancient Greece. In spite of, or perhaps because of the beautiful natural landscape with its dramatic and varied scenery, especially rich flora and the munificent climate, the Greeks (together with the Minoans) were the least ornamental garden-minded civilisations of the ancient world – even though they were latterly aware of the Persian *pairidaēza*. Gardens were made, for example the small Garden of Epicurus in Athens was laid out at a cost of 7060 drachmas (one drachma being a day's wages). Epicurus (341–270 BCE) lived there in a three-wheeled chair and willed the garden and house to his fellow philosophers. And, according to the Athenian speech-writer Isaeus in his *On the Estate of Dicaeogenes* (5.11), Leochares 'bought and demolished their ancestral house, and made the garden adjoining his own house in the city'. Nonetheless and in spite of the Athenian architectural invention of the peristyle courtyard, the overriding impression of Greek gardens is of mundane functionality.

However the Greeks had an extensive religio-mythology of which we have an exhaustive knowledge. The Greek belief system was polytheistic with twelve main gods and goddesses: Zeus, Hera, Aphrodite, Apollo, Ares, Artemis, Athena, Demeter, Dionysus, Hephaestus, Hermes and Poseidon, most of whom, together with dozens of lesser gods, dwelt on Mount Olympus. Just like the Mesopotamian deities the Greek ones had human form and supernatural powers, and the Greeks believed the origins of their world and its natural phenomena were all or in part explained through the lives and adventures of their many deities, heroes and

mythical beasts. Thus the Greeks had a real world vision, that is to say their world was a revered nature blessed by the gods, and the places associated with these gods were part (albeit a sometimes mythological part) of the physical world rather than somewhere 'out there' in the cosmos.

We are all familiar with Greek myths, many of which express the divine quality of the harmony of nature and/or have strong plant associations. For example, Dionysus the god of the vine, winemaking and wine was associated with the grape vine (of course), ivy (thought to negate drunkenness), fig (purgative) and pine (a wine preservative). His symbol was a *thyrsus* – a giant fennel stalk tipped with a pinecone – perhaps a wise choice since it would cause

LEFT Mainland Greece is blessed with a munificent climate, striking landscape and diverse flora. Under the nearest olive tree are asphodels, a plant that was said to dominate the Field of Asphodel in Hades, the Greek afterlife.

RIGHT Painted between 1470 and 1480 *Apollo and Daphne* by Piero Pollaiuolo shows the moment that the nymph, pursued by the sun god, called out to Gaia for help and was transformed into the shrub that bears her name.

minimal injury when wielded in a drunken cult activity. Another cult which involved the use of plant products was the Eleusinian Mysteries (the Cult of Demeter). Part of the initiation was the consumption of *kykeon*, a drink that induced a hallucinogenic or euphoric state and was possibly made from ergotized barley which produces LSD and ergonovine.

There are, too, numerous transformation or metamorphosis myths involving plants, for example Hyacinthus, Narcissus and Daphne, whilst the turning of the seasons and the growth of plants required the input of several deities. Chloris (from *chloe*, meaning 'the newly-born green shoot'), so beautifully depicted by Botticelli, personified spring. Artemis, the virgin goddess of the moon, revived the plants each night with her refreshing dew, while her twin brother Apollo, as the sun god, sent the sun's rays, essential for the well-being of the plants. The ripening of the fields and crops lay under the care of Demeter to whom wheat was sacred. Demeter's abdication of her fertility role when mourning the temporary loss of her daughter Persephone marked winter. Persephone was abducted by Hades – the god and the place shared the same name – to be his queen of the underworld. She was rescued but condemned to remain part of the year in the underworld, the length of her detention decided upon by the number of pomegranate seeds she had eaten in Hades – one month for every seed. Her return symbolised the germination process of plants because she re-emerged onto the earth each spring.

Hades itself was divided into three parts. First Tartarus, where evil and treacherous souls were sent and lived out eternity in horrible punishment. Then the Field of Asphodel, a less perfect version of earth inhabited by those whose lives were equally good and bad. This ghostly place was described

by Homer in the *Odyssey*, which dates to the eighth century BCE, as a great meadow covered with *Asphodelus albus* which have silver-grey foliage and white, spiky flowers. The flower as a symbol of death was also associated with Persephone who was often depicted crowned with a garland of the flowers. Lastly there was Elysium or the Elysian Fields where the souls of heroic and virtuous were to enjoy an immortality of bliss. It was described by Homer as a place, 'Where life is easiest for men. No snow is there, nor heavy storm, nor ever rain, but ever does Ocean send up blasts of the shrill-blowing West Wind that they may give cooling to men'. A more detailed description was given by Pindar in one of his *thrénoi* (dirges or songs of lamentation) and quoted by Plutarch in his *Moralia* (Letter to Apollonius 35,120c):

> For them doth the strength of the sun shine below,
> While night all the earth doth overstrow.
> In meadows of roses their suburbs lie,
> Roses all tinged with a crimson dye.
> They are shaded by trees that incense bear,
> And trees with golden fruit so fair.
> Some with horses and sports of might,
> Others in music and draughts delight.
> Happiness there grows ever apace,
> Perfumes are wafted o'er the loved place,
> As the incense they strew where the gods' altars are
> And the fire that consumes it is seen from afar.

Pindar also claims in his second Olympian ode (476 BCE) that those who dwell in Elysium will not remain there forever. Rather, after three lifetimes, the souls of the good are conveyed to the Islands of the Blessed, there to be rewarded with an everlasting happiness in a paradise where suffering and fear have been banished and where 'ocean breezes blow around the island of the blessed, and flowers of gold are blazing, some on the shore from radiant trees, while others the water fostereth; and with chaplets thereof they entwine their hands, and with crowns'. It may be that these islands were the Canary Islands which are out beyond the Pillars of Hercules (the Strait of Gibraltar), out in what the Greeks called the 'Unknown'. There is, too, a possible association between the Islands of the Blessed and the mythological, island-based Garden of Alcinous. Homer's description in the *Odyssey* gives more particulars of what the garden element of the Greek afterlife may have been expected to offer:

> Outside the gate of the outer court there is a large garden of about four acres with a wall all round it. It is full of beautiful trees — pears, pomegranates, and the most delicious apples. There are luscious figs also, and olives in full growth. The fruits never rot nor fail all the year round, neither winter nor summer, for the air is so soft that a new crop ripens before the old has dropped. Pear grows on pear, apple on apple, and fig on fig, and so also with the grapes, for there is an excellent vineyard: on the level ground of a part of this, the grapes are being made into raisins; in another part they are being gathered; some are being trodden in the wine tubs, others further on have shed their blossom and are beginning to show fruit, others again are just changing colour. In the furthest part of the ground there are beautifully arranged beds of flowers that are in bloom all the year round. Two streams go through it, the one turned in ducts throughout the whole garden, while the other is carried under the ground of the outer court to the house itself, and the town's people draw water from it. Such, then, were the splendours with which the gods had endowed the house of king Alcinous.

Wherever their location, both the Isles of the Blessed and Elysium are an idyllic afterlife and thus have strong similarities with the Egyptian Aaru and the Aztec Tlalocan — an afterlife paradise of unending springtime with an abundance of green foliage and edible plants, ruled over by Tlaloc. The Isles of the Blessed is also a phrase and similar concept that appears in pagan Celtic, Pure Land Buddhist and Taoist mythology. Parallels between this afterlife idyll may also be made with mankind's ages of innocence, for example the Greek Golden Age and the paradise gardens (as opposed to an idyllic rural landscape) described in the creation myths of the Sumerian Dilmun and the Judaeo-Christian Eden.

LEFT This third century AD Roman fresco from a hypogeum in the district of Octavia depicts Mercury, the messenger of the gods who is carrying his caduceus or herald's staff, standing in a floriferous Elysium, the Greek paradisiacal afterlife.

RIGHT With Hera holding one of the golden apples borne by the tree around which is twined the fearsome Ladon while the nymphs look on, this detail from a fourth-century BCE Greek vase captures the essence of the Garden of the Hesperides.

The 'Unknown', according to certain Roman sources, is also the location for Hera's orchard in the west, the Garden of the Hesperides. Within it grew a tree bearing immortality-giving golden apples (sometimes claimed to be oranges or quinces), a wedding gift to Hera and Zeus from Gaia. The three Hesperides were nymphs who tended the garden and Ladon a never-sleeping, hundred-headed dragon provided protection for the tree. Hercules for his Eleventh Labour was directed to steal one of the apples and they also appear in the myth of the first beauty pageant, or more correctly the Judgement of Paris. Aphrodite bribed Paris with Helen of Troy to 'fix' the result and judge her more beautiful than Hera and Athena. Rather than a tiara and rubbing salt into the wound,

LEFT This beautifully-worked, mid-fifth century BCE bell krater by the Eupolis Painter (an Athenian red-figure vase painter whose name is unknown) depicts the Judgement of Paris — the fateful event that led to all the troubles with Helen and the Greek destruction of Troy.

BELOW A hillside in Sithonia planted with perhaps the most symbolic of all Greek plants, the olive. Associated with Athena, the goddess of wisdom (and much more), a wreath made of it was the most sought-after prize at the early Olympic Games.

Paris presented Aphrodite with one of Hera's golden apples. The apple is similarly imbued with qualities of immortality in Norse mythology: the goddess Ithunn supplied gods with apples that provided eternal youth; and of course the apple is associated with the forbidden fruit of the garden in Eden.

In the 'real world' plants played a symbolic role at the Olympic Games which were held at sacred Olympia, one of the largest Greek sanctuaries and equal in importance to Delphi. Although the origin of the Olympic Games is lost, it was certainly religious. The games assumed a pan-Hellenic character in 776 BCE and garlands were established as the official, symbolic awards and the highest accolade was an olive wreath. The olive was sacred to Athena the goddess of peace, a busy goddess who was also responsible for wisdom, triumph, courage, inspiration, civilisation, law and justice, just warfare, mathematics, strength, strategy, the arts, crafts, and skill. Thus as well as being an emblem of triumph the victor's garland — made from the wild olive tree which legend had it Hercules brought from the land of the Hyperborean and planted at Olympia — was representative of Athena's attributes.

Physical training for games would have been a part of the educational syllabus taught at the famous Athenian gymnasia:

ABOVE The ruins of the once splendid amphitheatre at Dodona. According to the historian Herodotus the shrine here was the oldest Hellenic oracle, possibly dating to the second millennium BCE.

TOP Dating to 330 BCE the Temple of Zeus once dominated the centre of the Sanctuary of Zeus at Nemea which was planted with cypress trees.

Plato's Academy, Aristotle's Lyceum and Antisthenes's Cynosarges. Each of these establishments was dedicated to a deity whose statue adorned the structure and surrounding the buildings were groves with avenues and shady *peripatoi* or walks used during academic instruction. Particularly praised were the groves of plane (*Platanus orientalis*), elm (*Ulmus glabra*) and poplar (*Populus alba*) trees at the Academy, the grounds of which also contained an ancient grove of olives sacred to Athena, the city's goddess. But, as occurred during the wars that beset Mesopotamia when conquering armies felled sacred groves, so too were the trees of both the Academy and Lyceum destroyed by the Roman general Sulla during the siege of Athens in 86 BCE.

Gods and goddesses were worshipped at cult sites, for example a particularly beautiful and revered spring or mountain, as well as at constructed shrines, sanctuaries and in temples often planted round with sacred groves. As we shall see in the next chapter, some two millennia later and in Britain this arrangement of classical architecture set amid planted stands of trees was to become a core element of the eighteenth-century picturesque landscapes of William Kent. Evidence for the groves and gardens associated with temples

and sanctuaries comes from both literature and the archaeological record but details are frustratingly scanty. Reputed to be the first site of oracular divination, Dodona at Epeiros in north west Greece was sacred to Zeus Dodoneas and here prophesy was delivered via the rustling of the branches of the sacred oak tree. A late fourth-century BCE inscription from the island of Thasos tells of a garden planted with myrtle (*Myrtus communis*), fig and nut trees belonging to a temple of Hercules; and the cypress grove mentioned by Pausanius surrounding the temple of Zeus at Nemea in the north eastern Peloponnese is backed up by archaeological evidence of twenty-three tree pits cut into bed rock. Similar pits were discovered around the temple of Hephaestus in the Athenian agora. The sanctuary of Aphrodite at Palaepaphos on Cyprus was one of most important pilgrimage sites in ancient Greece. In c.22 BCE the Greek geographer Strabo in his *Geographia* (14, 6) recounts that an annual festival of Aphrodite, the goddess of love and to whom the rose and apples were sacred, involved a procession from Nea Paphos to Palaepaphos which passed through the sanctuary and sacred grove of Apollo Hylates and the 'Hierokepis', the sacred gardens of Aphrodite. Regrettably Strabo gives no further details of the garden itself.

LEFT A spectacular show of red poppy anemone, the plant which was supposed to have sprung up from the blood of the mortally-wounded Adonis.

RIGHT A red-figure lekythos depicts Aphrodite receiving an Adonis garden from a winged Eros. She will ascend the stairway and place the planted broken potsherd on the roof of the house.

There is, however, a link between the two deities, for at least some of the aspects of Apollo worshipped on Cyprus can be traced to an indigenous male deity of vegetation and fertility. In another guise this companion of Aphrodite became known as Adonis. During the Cypriote festival of 'Aoia' which refers to the goddess's companion, trees were cut and sacrificed to Aphrodite. Similarly, the scene of Adonis's death was a grove, and Aphrodite's desperate search for his body culminated with its discovery on Cyprus and within Erithios, a sacred grove of Apollo.

The youthful, beautiful Adonis from whose spilled blood Aphrodite created *Anemone coronaria* was also central to one form of religio-symbolic garden-making undertaken annually by the women of Athens (both citizen and non-citizen alike) during the festival of Adonia. Whilst not recognised officially as a state festival by the deeply androcentric Athenian society, it is clear from Aristophanes's *Lysistrata* (the play was presented in 411 BCE) that the privately celebrated Adonia was a boisterous affair, mourning Adonis with lament, dancing and drinking over a day and a night. One aspect mentioned by Menander in his *Samia* (308 BCE) and described by Plato in his *Phaedrus* (370 BCE) were the 'gardens of Adonis' created specifically for the festival and which the celebrating women carried up to the roof of the house. From other sources we learn that these gardens consisted of pots and/or potsherds filled with earth and sown with quickly-germinating seeds, perhaps lettuce, for according to Euboulos (a fourth-century BCE comic poet) Aphrodite herself laid out the body of her dead lover in a bed of lettuce. The exact meaning of the gardens has been lost, but interpretations generally agree on a death and mourning symbolism, ranging from the quick death of these unwatered seedlings being analogous to Adonis's premature demise to the pots/sherds being a bier for Adonis dolls, the latter described as part of the festival by Plutarch. Some commentators have suggested that the 'pleasant gardens' referred to in the Book of Isaiah (17.10) may indeed be Adonis gardens. Be that as it may, this is one aspect of Greek mythology that has a clear parallel with the Judaeo-Christian creation myth of the Garden in Eden (explored in more detail in the next chapter). The Golden Age was a time on earth that occurred before the invention of the arts and ownership of private property, when nature produced food in such abundance that there was no need for agriculture. A time when humans, according to Hesiod in his *Works and Days*:

> lived like gods without sorrow of heart, remote and free from toil and grief: miserable age rested not on them . . . and they had all good things; for the fruitful earth unforced bare them fruit abundantly and without stint. They dwelt in ease and peace upon their lands, with many good things, rich in flocks and loved by the blessed gods.

The etiology of Eden is remarkably similar and in both cases one explanation is that this was the perceived 'paradise' when nature provided for mankind before his transition from hunter-gatherer to an agrarian lifestyle.

# Rome

At its largest in AD 117 the Roman Empire covered 6.8 million square kilometres (2.6 million square miles) and boasted a population of 70 millions. Worldly, urbane and practical, the Romans also considered themselves highly religious and attributed their success and power to their collective *pietas* (piety) in maintaining good relations with the gods. They also adopted a typically pragmatic attitude to religion: a contractual relationship in which man revered, worshipped and provided sacrifice and offerings to the gods and goddesses who were believed to control people's existence and who in return were expected to do the right thing and ensure Roman well-being. The practicalities were conducted as a combination of private, domestic devotion overseen by the *pater familias* (head of the family) and the state cult of public ceremonial, the responsibility for which resided with the official priesthood. Polytheistic as it was, Roman religion was not based on any central belief but was an admixture of rituals and traditions, taboos and superstitions that originated in the old religions of the Etruscans and Latin tribes and which had amalgamated down the centuries with other influences from Greek colonies.

However, by the third century BCE the Romans began to adopt a renamed and slightly adapted version of the Greek pantheon. For example, Flora was the Roman incarnation of Chloris, Ceres of Demeter, Bacchus of Dionysus, and Venus of Aphrodite who took on additional responsibility as goddess of the garden. Priapus kept his Greek name but assumed the role of god of edible crops and fertility in gardens. And in addition to the dozen Olympians and their multifarious relatives the Romans also raised a number of vegetative and horticultural deities of their own, including Pomona the goddess of fruit and Robigus the god of mildew (fungal infection of crops).

As well as religion and art, Ancient Rome also adopted Greek architectural style, including the peristyle courtyard enclosed within the structure of the house. But whereas in Classical Greece this had generally been a paved court in the Roman *domus* (town house) and the larger *villa urbana* (rural house) and *villa suburbana* (house near to or within a city) the space was transformed into a garden. The eruption of Vesuvius in AD 79 that buried Pompeii in ash and Herculaneum in mud has preserved a huge amount of

BELOW This villa garden unearthed and restored at Herculaneum shows the peristyle enclosing the garden space which is further defined by the box hedge.

RIGHT With its fresh green background this most delightful fresco from the Villa di Arianna at Stabia shows beautiful Flora, goddess of spring imbuing plants — in this case oleander — with new life.

archaeological evidence pertaining to Roman gardens of the first century, and this is augmented by earlier discoveries from all over the empire. One of the most famous of the Pompeiian town house gardens is that of the House of the Vettii, owned by two rich freedmen brothers who ornamented the garden extensively. And although much remains encased in mud the much larger Villa of the Papyri at Herculaneum provided the inspiration for the Getty Villa in Pacific Palisades, California which contains four authentically recreated Roman gardens. The villa itself is a reconstruction based on the (still continuing) excavation of the Villa dei Papiri or Villa of the Papyri at Herculaneum which was engulfed by volcanic pyroclastic flows in AD 79. Integrated within and around the substantial building are four delightful gardens designed by Denis Kurutz, Matt Randolph and Amy Korn. They aim to provide an insight into the form and planting of gardens made in the 1st century AD by a wealthy patron.

The largest and most impressive garden is the Outer Peristyle entered via the villa's south doors and which in true

BELOW AND OPPOSITE Two views of the very impressive Outer Peristyle garden at the Getty Villa in Pacific Palisades, California. Both garden and villa are a reproduction based on the excavation of the Villa of the Papyri at Herculaneum, and the garden contains a comprehensive collection of those sacro-religious ornaments and plants favoured by first-century AD Roman garden makers.

villa marittima fashion boasts splendid views of the Pacific Ocean beyond. The walls of the peristyle are painted with religio-symbolic *oscilla* and garlands (Romans would have used living flowers to make such garlands and the *oscilla* would have been cast in clay and hung as ornaments). Two pergolas link the paved peristyle walk to the garden. The formal garden of individual flower beds enclosed by low clipped box hedges and separated by gravel paths is arranged around the central, 67-metre-long (73 yards) reflecting pool. The bronze statues and herms are replicas of those found at the Villa dei Papiri and the garden also features circular stone seats and plants in large terracotta pots.

Statuary is also important in the smaller Inner Peristyle, a slightly sunken, square courtyard within the centre of the villa complex on to which the ground floor rooms open. Here too is a narrow rectangular pool with small jets that is aligned on the nymphaeum, a colourful, mosaic-and-shell fountain in the East Garden. This third garden is shaded by sycamore and laurel trees and also features a central circular pool into which water falls from sculpted bronze civet heads set within a raised bowl. The fourth garden to the west of the villa is a large productive garden planted with 'period correct' fruits, vegetables

and herbs favoured by the Romans and which would have been used not only in the kitchen but also for domestic and medicinal purposes as well as for religious ceremony and ritual.

The peristyle garden was a space designed for relaxation and a display of conspicuous consumption, but also for *otium*, the concept of withdrawing from one's daily business or affairs (*negotium*) to engage in activities that were considered to be artistically valuable or enlightening (for example oratory, writing, philosophy) as well as religious observance. Surrounded by the peristyle which provided shelter from inclement weather and the sun these gardens were formal in design. Either at ground level or sometimes sunken, the space was occupied by flower beds defined by neatly-clipped low evergreen hedges (often of box, *Buxus sempervirens*). Paths of gravel or stone paving led between the beds and ornament included water features and pools, seating and couches for *al fresco* dining as well as features that had a religious symbolism. The ever-practical Romans often painted the enclosing walls of the peristyle with *trompe l'oeil* murals of sacro-religious natural landscape scenes that simultaneously made the garden space seem larger. Certain ornamentation had a religious overtone, for example the choice of statuary and herms (statues consisting of a squared pillar displaying

genitalia crowned with a carved head) focused on garden-related deities which in addition to those mentioned included Hercules (in relation to his Eleventh Labour) and Pan. Statues sometimes doubled as fountains, while nymphs were venerated in a *nymphaeum*, a small ornamental building or structure which was often designed as a water feature. Such structures evolved from natural grottoes and imitation naturalistic grottoes were sometimes manufactured in the landscapes surrounding larger country villa gardens. Here too small temples could be found set within groves.

To provide all-year-round interest in the flower beds evergreen plants were widely used, especially those with a symbolic quality, for example ivy (Bacchus), laurel (*Laurus nobilis*, Apollo), myrtle and rose (Venus). Other popular evergreens included arbutus, date palm, oleander and viburnum. Fruit trees were also a firm favourite: apple, cherry, damson,

fig, peach, pear, yellow and blue plum, pomegranate and, if one could afford it, citrus. Flower beds also provided plant material for coronary wreaths which lost their purely honorific status as time went by and became worn on the person as well as adorning garden statuary. They were made from strands of ivy, sarsaparilla (*Smilax aspera*) or vine interwoven with seasonal flowers and foliage and there were variously named types, for example the *cosmosandala* was ornamented with narcissus, lily, rose and larkspur. Longer, larger garland swags were strung between the pillars of the peristyle, between which also dangled *oscilla* — terracotta masks or faces hung as offerings to various deities.

BELOW A fresco from the triclinium in the Roman house of Livia, 20–10 BC. The fresco was originally in a vaulted ,underground room and shows an ideal garden, with flowers, trees and birds.

RIGHT A detail of a flower garland strung between the pillars of the peristyle from a fresco found in the House of Livia, Rome.

BELOW The Mausoleum of Augustus in Rome from an eighteenth-century print which shows a formal garden made within and the walls covered in climbing plants.

One aspect of the Greek belief system the Romans did not adopt was the Hadean afterlife. Romans valued and enjoyed gardens in life and believed the ghosts of their deceased ancestors enjoyed the gardens laid out for them around their tombs. Many epitaphs mentioning gardens have survived from tombs: 'Sprinkle my ashes with pure wine and fragrant oil of spikenard; bring balsam, too, stranger with red roses. Unending spring pervades my tearless urn. I have not died, but changed my state.' (Ausonias, Epitaphs 31).

Unfortunately not so the tombs and gardens themselves. Nevertheless an indication of their layout may be gleaned from an engraved marble slab from a cemetery on the Via Labicana in Rome. It depicts a stylised plan of a funerary monument with formal gardens in front of the tomb comprising a series of square and rectangular flower beds separated by a small grove of trees planted in rows. One monumental funerary monument has survived, at least partially intact. The Mausoleum of Augustus, which the emperor began in 31 BCE upon his return to Rome after victory over Mark Anthony and Cleopatra in Egypt, was inspired by his visit to the tomb of Alexander the Great in Alexandria. Built on the northern edge of the Campus Martius the circular structure with a diameter of almost 80 metres (87 yards) and height of 44 metres (48 yards) was itself described by Strabo as 'thickly covered with evergreen trees' – an echo perhaps of the tomb of Osiris – and set within a public park where, according to Suetonius, Augustus 'opened to the public the groves and walks by which it was surrounded'. And now, two thousand years after the emperor's death, his mausoleum is about to undergo a major restoration.

# Abrahamic religions

## Eden

In the Christian faith heaven is a transcendental realm, a place of happiness in which the repentant who have died on earth continue to exist in an afterlife. The New Testament does make an association between 'paradise' and the realm of the blessed dead but this is considered by scholars to be the result of literary Hellenistic influences. The word 'paradise' also occurs three times in the Old Testament: the Song of Solomon (4.13), Ecclesiastes (2.5) and Nehemiah (2.8), but in each case what is being described is a man-made rather than a divine garden and the etymology comes from the *pairidaēza* of Persia. Therefore, and unlike Islam, there are very few indicators that the Christian afterlife takes place in a garden setting.

Jewish sacred texts and literature have relatively little to say about what happens after death but there are some somewhat confusing references to 'Gan Eden' (the Garden in Eden) as a paradisiacal afterlife. Talmudic teachings, however, discuss Gan Eden as an earthly paradise and part of the Judaeo-Christian creation narrative that idealises prehistory, a time when God through his divinely-created nature spontaneously provided man with all his needs:

And the Lord God planted a garden eastward in Eden; and there he put the man whom he had formed. And out of the ground made the Lord God to grow every tree that is pleasant to the sight, and good for food; the tree of life also in the midst of the garden, and the tree of knowledge of good and evil. And a river went out of Eden to water the garden; and from thence it was parted, and became into four heads. The name of the first is Pison: that is it which compasseth the whole land of Havilah, where there is gold; And the gold of that land is good: there is bdellium and the onyx stone. And the name of the second river is Gihon: the same is it that compasseth the whole land of Ethiopia. And the name of the third river is Tigris: that is it which goeth toward the east of Assyria. And the fourth river is Euphrates. And the Lord God took the man, and put him into the garden of Eden to dress it and to keep it. And the Lord God commanded the man, saying, Of every tree of the garden thou mayest freely eat: But of the tree of the knowledge of good and evil, thou shalt not eat of it: for in the day that thou eatest thereof thou shalt surely die.
Genesis 2: 8–17

The very first verse specifically speaks about a garden *in* Eden which denotes the larger territory within which was an enclosed garden. If we examine the actual characteristics of the garden they are modest enough. Well-watered by a stream that became the headwaters of the four rivers this was a place for God to take an evening stroll among all kinds of beautiful trees producing delicious fruits and peaceful animals and birds. The Book of Ezekiel (28.13 and 31.8) adds a very

LEFT Choosing a subject always popular with religious painters, Lucas Cranach the Elder depicts a much more expansive Eden complete with fauna in his *Adam and Eve in the Garden of Eden*, 1530.

OPPOSITE From the *Très Riches Heures du Duc de Berry* by Pol de Limbourg. This delightful painting shows God, Adam and Eve in an enclosed and verdant Garden in Eden with its two important trees and the source of the river (the large fountain).

Sumerian touch calling Eden, 'the garden of God' which, like the Gilgameshian garden of the gods, was full of precious gems and where there grew a cedar more beautiful than any other tree in Eden. In this case however the tree was not felled by a demi-god and his hooligan accomplice but another tree, the Tree of the Knowledge of Good and Evil bore the fruit that Adam ate of, the act which caused the Fall of Man. There is a consensus that the fruit consumed was not an apple because the tree is not native to the Tigris and Euphrates river basins. An alternative suggestion is the apricot which has long been regarded as an erotic and sensuous fruit, and at times an aphrodisiac. The other significant plants in the creation narrative are the Tree of Life whose fruit gave immortality and the fig tree with whose leaves Adam and Eve hid their nakedness after the Fall.

While the garden form is relatively uncomplicated, the etiology of Eden itself is far more complex and embraces a number of issues including the creation of man and woman, of vegetation and animals, the origin of language, and, in contrast with the Sumerian creation myth, the prohibition of incest. Similarly to the Greek Golden Age, the narrative idealises a time when nature spontaneously provided mankind with all his needs, but emphasises that the cause of the Fall was the impulse of human ambition to be like God. Man's expulsion, his emergence into history and the beginnings of culture are forced on him by the withdrawal of nature's bounty, the loss of paradise. Could this narrative in fact be a metaphor for the shift from hunter-gatherer to agrarian lifestyle? Certainly it would fit with one of the suggested locations for Eden, which for almost three millennia Jews and Christians believed was a physical place on earth. The Agricultural Revolution occurred about 10,000 years ago in the Fertile Crescent and one hypothesis is that Eden was located under the headwaters of the Persian Gulf and submerged as sea levels rose following the last Ice Age. Other suggested locations include the island of Bahrain, the same setting as is sometimes identified for the Sumerian Dilmun; an area referred to in Sumerian texts as the Edin (literally 'plain') beyond the Zagros mountains north of Mesopotamia, and, for completeness-sake and according to Mormon theology, Independence in Missouri.

Many of the plants named in the Bible, for example the acacia tree (above) were considered to be God-given inasmuch as they are useful and provide for the needs of mankind. The palm too (left) is so revered but in this sixth-century AD mosaic from a synagogue it probably represents the Edenic Tree of the Knowledge of Good and Evil and the Tree of Life.

# Plants of the Bible

Although God withdrew from man nature's spontaneous provision it was believed that (as in many other belief systems, for example that of Ancient Greece) many useful and important plants were God-given. In the Book of Isaiah for example God states that (and translations vary), 'I will plant in the wilderness the cedar, the acacia tree, and the myrtle, and the olive tree; I will set in the desert the juniper tree, and the pine, and cypress box tree together' (41:19). Solomon's Temple was constructed from cedar and both the Tabernacle of the Ark of the Covenant and Noah's Ark were built from acacia. Noah also became the first human to plant a vineyard and become drunk on his wine (Genesis 9:20). Indeed, about half of the over 240 taxa identifiable in the Bible were utilised as foodstuffs, spices and condiments, cosmetics, drugs and medicines, were processed into textiles, used for fuel and building or had a domestic application. Deuteronomy reveals that the Land of Israel was blessed with wheat, barley, figs, dates, pomegranates, vines and the olive (8:8). The latter was supremely useful, providing timber, fruits to eat and oil which was variously used to cook, to burn for light and to provide the base for perfumed oils. A recipe given in Exodus includes myrrh, cinnamon and cassia (30: 23–24). Myrrh and another spice, frankincense, were of course gifts brought to Bethlehem for the baby Jesus (who lay in a manger filled with straw) and are two of many examples of symbolic plants that appear in the New Testament. Later in life Mary Magdalene applied spikenard perfume when she washed Jesus's feet with her hair. When Jesus descended from the Mount of Olives to enter Jerusalem in triumph people lay down small tree or palm branches (as well as their clothes) in front of him along his route. At the end of his life Jesus was mocked as King of the Jews and given a crown of thorns (traditionally said to be of *Sarcopoterium spinosum*). He was nailed to a wooden cross and buried in the Garden of Gethsemane wrapped in a shroud of linen.

Yet of all the many plant references in the New Testament the most frequently mentioned and most featured in parable is the vine. Jesus claimed, 'I am the true Vine' and John (2:1–11) recounts his first the miracle at a wedding in Cana when Jesus transformed water into wine, and wine continues metaphysically to represent the blood of Christ during the Eucharist.

# Medieval gardens

Within the Judaeo-Christian faith as it emerged and consolidated in the Holy Land there was not the garden-making tradition seen in Egypt or Mesopotamia. Indeed it was not until after the collapse of the Western Roman Empire (from AD 476) and several centuries following Christianity's arrival in northern Europe that a Christian garden form emerged. The misnomered Dark Ages saw artistic expression of a high level but also a return to insularity and localism. But there was one group of men within society who did travel, who proselyted and who were the repositories of learning and horticultural skills – monks. The ascetic (or supposedly so) monastic lifestyle demanded self-sufficiency and monastery gardens were therefore by and large utilitarian. The one exception was the cloister with its 'garth' (plural 'garthen', meaning 'enclosed space' and the origin of the word garden).

Saint Bernard (Bernard of Clairvaux, 1090–1153), one of the key figures in the establishment of the Cistercian order, exclaimed, 'Truly, the cloister is a paradise, a realm protected by the rampart of a discipline that contains a rich abundance of priceless treasures'. In many ways this enclosed, protected, innocent and holy place to which only pure-of-soul monks had access had a strong resonance with Eden and was considered a form of earthly paradise. Such an implication was made explicit by Herrad of Landsberg (d.1195), abbess of Sainte-Odile in Alsace. In her spiritual anthology *Hortus deliciarum* she categorised the phrase 'the earthly paradise' to mean (either alone or in combination) the Christian soul, a pure conscience, virginity, heavenly Jerusalem, the Church watered by the four streams of the gospels, monastic life and the cloister.

The medieval monastic cloister was considered to be an encapsulation of Eden. In the centre (left of picture opposite) of an intimate cloister within the twelfth-century Cistercian Abbey of Fontfroide near Narbonne, France is a well which represented the river that 'went out of Eden', and within the quiet confines of a cloister such as that at Royaumont Abbey of Asnières-sur-Oise (above) monks would have studied and contemplated.

The architectural form of the cloister owed much to the Greek peristyle courtyard but the garden within emphasised the overtones of Eden. The walled-in space redolent with God's presence was frequently planted with an evergreen tree to symbolise the Tree of Life (or Christ's Cross). A well or fountain was symbolic of the 'river [that] went out of Eden to water the garden; and from thence it was parted and became into four heads' and the garden space itself sometimes symbolised these four rivers by a quadripartite division. A similarly representative motif but with a different symbolism is found in the Islamic *chahar bagh* garden form (see p.72). The cloister's purpose as a place of religious learning, spiritual contemplation and devotional praise has faint echoes of both the Greek gymnasium and Roman *otium*; while the medieval Church as an institution assumed the metaphysical representation of paradise. This significant step saw the Church establish itself in the powerful position as the *only*

vehicle through which the redeemed penitent had access
to Christ and could regain Eden.

From the seventh century onwards the cult of the Virgin
Mary became more influential within the Church. Various
plants became emblematic of her virtues, for example the
red rose, once sacred to Venus now became Mary's flower
(red roses also represented the blood of martyrs), the violet
(*Viola odorata*) reflected her humility and the white petals
of the Madonna lily represented her purity while its golden
anthers showed the glowing light of her soul.

Mary also became allegorically linked with a second form
of monastic garden, the enclosed garden or *hortus conclusus*.
One of the earliest known examples of a garden specifically
dedicated to Mary was created by the Irish Saint Fiacre in
the mid-seventh century. Somewhat bizarrely too, the cult
of Mary became entwined with the medieval allegorical
interpretation of the Old Testament book, the Song of
Songs. This lyrical poem conducted between a woman and
a man often identified as King Solomon is filled with erotic
energy and imagery that draws heavily on the language of
landscape and nature, where, for example, pomegranates,
asphodels and lilies are all used in similes to describe
the beloved. By the twelfth century the new reading had
identified Mary as the 'beloved' of Solomon and had led
to her depiction in the *hortus conclusus*. Moreover, Mary
metaphysically became a fecund garden because of what grew
within her (Jesus), a closed garden because she is fruitful to
God alone, and a garden in which she is also the fountain
in a spiritual sense, providing the font of life.

'The Little Garden of Paradise' (1430) by an unknown
artist from the Upper Rhine captures this allegory and the
form of the *hortus conclusus* perfectly. A crenellated wall
surrounds a garden rich with diverse flowers including
the Madonna lily, a red peony, blue iris, lily-of-the-valley,
carnations and strawberry planted both in raised beds and
studded into the sward in a style known as 'flowery mead'.
A maid scoops water from a tank which could represent the
fountain of life. Depicted in contemporary costume as if they
are lords and ladies are Saint Michael conversing with Saint
George (who has dispatched the world's most feeble dragon
that lies talons up amongst the flowers) while Jesus plays

Saint Cecilia's lyre, and a composed Mary, seated perhaps
on a turf seat, quietly reads. It was also in the fifteenth
century that such *hortus conclusus* gardens acquired the
name 'Mary gardens', the first reference to which is an
account for plants by the sacristan of Norwich Priory. In
the past couple of decades there has been a revival of Mary
gardens. Today they have lost their deep symbolism and are
most often a collection of plants with a Mary or biblical
connection (see p.193).

RIGHT The Madonna lily is one of the plants that became associated with Mary in medieval times. Since then many more have become 'Mary flowers'.

BELOW 'The Little Garden of Paradise' as described in the text opposite. Do note the feeble dragon that St George has bravely slain!

Within secular medieval literature, for example the French poem 'Le Roman de la Rose' (composed 1230–75) and Boccaccio's *Teseida* (before 1341 and the inspiration for Chaucer's *The Knight's Tale*) the *hortus conclusus* was remodelled as a setting for courtly love. Found within castle walls or just outside, the physical manifestation of such knightly, chivalrous gardens boasted turf seats and fountains, bowers and arbours, lawns and flowery meads, raised beds filled with scented flowers and fruit-laden trees. They were delightful and charming hideaways, secluded and verdant retreats for lovers, or places for courtly entertainments and revelry. The development of the secular garden as romantic retreat is likely to have also been influenced by the gardens that Crusaders encountered in the Holy Land and/or the gardens of Al-Andalus on the Iberian peninsula. For even if they did not perhaps understand the religious connotations of the gardens of Islam, royal and knightly garden-makers would no doubt have been responsive to these delightful paradise gardens.

Three medieval paintings showing how the religious *hortus conclusus* became adapted in the secular world of the monarchy and nobility as a garden of pleasure, beauty and romance. Two lovers (opposite page) share an intimate moment in the garden of a castle. A party (above) enjoy a courtly garden as a setting for revelry in an illustration from 'Le Roman de la Rose' and (below) Maugis and Orlando hold a conversation in the Garden of Love, from Liedet's 'Renaud de Montauban' cycle.

# The Cloisters Museum and Gardens

## New York, USA

New York may not be the first destination that springs to mind if one wishes to visit a medieval church cloister garden. However, a medieval style museum building, The Cloisters, was built between 1934 and 1939 in north Manhattan's Fort Tryon Park. This branch of the Metropolitan Museum of Art is devoted to medieval art and the building itself, designed by Charles Collens, incorporates original architectural elements dating from the twelfth to the fifteenth centuries. Importantly, the building also includes four cloisters which also contain original architectural elements from various French abbeys as well as ornaments of wider European origin.

The centrally positioned Cuxa Cloister is the largest and was reconstructed with fragments from the twelfth-century cloister of the Benedictine monastery of Saint-Michel-de-Cuxa in the north-east Pyrenees. It also contains the main ornamental garden, which, with a fountain bowl at its centre and divided into quarters by perpendicular stone-flagged paths, has a traditional monastic garth form. However, the planting includes modern cultivars as well as medieval species and for accuracy's-sake it must be noted that plantings of this style would have been found within the monastery's utilitarian gardens and not in the cloister. Similarly the Bonnefont

Cloister, which features delicate stonework originally thought to have come from a Cistercian monastery in Bonnefont-en-Comminges near Toulouse but now identified as from a late thrirteenth-century Franciscan monastery in Tarbes, contains historically-inaccurate raised beds. These and the 250 period-correct utilitarian herbs planted there would have been found in the hospital garden and the herbs would have been used in cooking and for medicines and domestic purposes. The Trie Cloister, which includes elements from the cloister of the Carmelite convent of Trie-en-Bigorre also near Toulouse, again boasts a central fountain while the planting is inspired

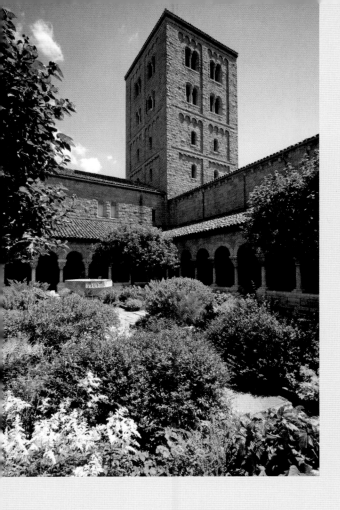

RIGHT The Trie Cloister boasts an ornate central fountain and whilst the planting makes use of 'period correct' taxa the riot of plants that is the planting design would not have been seen in a medieval cloister garth.

by European medieval images of fields, meadows and woodlands. And the fourth, the Saint-Guilhem Cloister is reconstructed with 140 late twelfth-century fragments from the Benedictine abbey of Saint-Guilhem-le-Désert, north west of Montpellier. With its central fountain, stone and gravel surfacing and pots in plants this space has a strong Islamic feel to it.

In spite of some of the liberties taken with the planting styles, the architecturally-accurate four cloisters provide a fascinating insight into medieval church gardening, both sacro-religious and utilitarian.

LEFT, ABOVE RIGHT and OVERLEAF The Cuxa Cloister is the largest of the four reconstructed cloisters within the museum complex. It has a form with a central fountain which is symbolic of the river source in Eden which branched to become the rivers Pison, Gihon, Tigris and Euphrates. The view of the belfry (above left) is from the Cuxa Cloister.

# Islam

The Prophet Muhammad states that 'God is beautiful and he loves beauty'. Thus to Muslims beauty is synonymous with Creation and anyone who contributes to the beauty of Creation is blessed. The Islamic garden is the most sophisticated expression of the combination of art, religion and beauty, a perfect harmony and unity between nature, man and God. Indeed, no other religion extols the beauties and pleasures of the garden as does Islam, and if we accept that for the sake of argument Buddhism is a religion then the Qur'an is only one of two religious texts that specifically describes the afterlife as a planned and functional paradise garden. The Gardens of Paradise or *Jannat al-Firdaws* are the highest level of paradise promised to the faithful believer as a heavenly reward: 'But those who have faith and work righteousness, they are companions of the Garden: Therein shall they abide' (2:82).

The Qur'an contains over 120 references to *Jannah* or paradise (the word means the same in this context as 'garden') and taken together with the descriptions in the Hadiths (sayings of the Prophet) and traditional Tafsīr (exegesis) provides a detailed account of the Muslim paradise. Given the religion's origins and development in the sun-parched, arid and dusty deserts of Arabia, it is not perhaps surprising that the Islamic notion of paradise is quite the opposite. It is a place of immortal bliss, free of care and pain, where the faithful wear the finest robes, perfumes and jewellery, enjoy a permanently munificent climate, inhabit palaces of gold, silver and pearl, recline on couches inlaid with gold or precious stones and partake of exquisite banquets, served in priceless vessels by immortal youths. All this is enjoyed within verdant and lofty gardens shaded by large trees, enlivened by fountains scented with camphor or ginger, enriched by delicious fruits of all kinds and seasons, all borne on trees without thorns. And running through the valleys

are 'rivers of water incorruptible; rivers of milk of which the taste never changes; rivers of wine, a joy to those who drink; and rivers of honey pure and clear' (47.15).

According to the traditional Islamic view, the Qur'an began in AD 610 with revelations to Muhammad in what is now Saudi Arabia. The rise of Islam was swift and in AD 734 Al-Mansur, the second Abbasid caliph (the caliphate was founded by the descendants of Muhammad's youngest uncle) established his new capital at Baghdad in what was then Persia. Construction took four years and in its early years the city was known as a deliberate reminder of an expression in the Qur'an, when it refers to Paradise. As we have seen, for centuries before the arrival of the Muslim invaders, Persia

RIGHT Showing a naturalistic scene rather than the prescribed *chahar bagh* quadripartite layout this Persian Folio from Haft Awrang (Seven Thrones) by Jami (1550s) shows how exotic Islamic gardens were and are typically hidden behind a humble exterior.

میان عرب و جنوب باغ خوض است و در دمی اپت اطراف انتم
درختهای نارنج اپت درختهای نارمهم است کرد اکر دوض تام
سبزکرزراست جای عین باغ امنیت در وقت زر دشن
نارهای بسیار خوب می باید ومیکی باغ خوبی طرح شده وطر

Often painted with a brush of a single hair one of the art forms popularised by the Mughals was incredibly detailed miniature painting. These scenes show themes on the *chahar bagh* with a raised, central water source feeding the four rills (above) and a seating area (left) that emphasises the importance of the garden's owner.

had developed and enjoyed a long and highly sophisticated garden-making tradition. The Persian model of a geometric four-fold garden divided by rills of running water, ornamented with fountains and richly planted had had its genesis in the palace gardens at Pasargadae and down the centuries became widely emulated. Realising that this established idiom accorded well with the Qur'anic description of paradise and thus provided a readily accessible template, the conquerors slowly adopted and adapted the Persian legacy and began to develop an Islamic garden form. However, according to Fairchild Ruggles in her *Islamic Gardens and Landscapes*, 'there is no evidence in the first four centuries of Islam that gardens were consciously designed with four quadrants

and four water channels in order to imitate paradise as the Qur'an described it'.

Nevertheless an early example, described by Jonas Benzion Lehrman in *Earthly Paradise: Garden and Courtyard in Islam*, was the Bulkawara or Balkowara Palace built between AD 849 and 859 at Samarra (a city that briefly replaced Baghdad as the capital between AD 838 and 892) which contained a series of quadripartite courts and gardens integral within the architecture of the palace. The quadripartite 'paradise blueprint' that eventually emerged was and is generically referred to by its Persian name *chahar bagh* or *charbagh* meaning 'four gardens'. It is a particularly adaptable blueprint and ingenious designers created earthly paradises across the Islamic world

from Umayyad Al-Andalus to Mughal India. And while the new garden form had a profound religious symbolism, this highly structured geometrical garden also 'became a powerful metaphor for the organisation and domestication of the landscape, itself a symbol of political territory' according to Ruggles. While such territorial displays are no longer relevant, the garden form and its symbolism certainly are. The *chahar bagh* with its delightful attention to beauty and detail continues to be the cornerstone of Islamic garden design today, from the rooftop of the Ismaili Centre in London to the al-Azhar Park in Cairo and contemporary gardens being made in the Gulf States and Indonesia.

Emperor Babur surveys the layout of Bagh-i Vafa (The Gardens of Fidelity), one of ten gardens he had made in Kabul. His body now resides in Bagh-i-Babur which he commissioned in 1528 and which has recently been restored.

This earthly paradise varies in form but not meaning. Small, private gardens are hidden behind tall walls that shut out the heat and prying eyes and deliberately present a humble exterior. A similar effect is created when courtyard gardens are closely integrated with the architecture of larger buildings such as within the Alhambra. Larger gardens like those in Kashmir and Kabul use the borrowed landscapes that their topography allows, while tomb gardens such as the Taj Mahal were designed to be expansive and a site of pilgrimage. Yet always the *chahar bagh* form is present. At its most straightforward it is a square space with four straight paths and/or rills that intersect at the centre and divide the space into four beds. Where there are rills the water flows from a central water source that may also feed bubbling fountains and sparkling jets that enliven the garden with sound and movement designed simultaneously to soothe the senses and cool the air.

The Alhambra or Red Fort was the fortified palatine city of the Nasrid dynasty (1232–1492). Perched on a plateau overlooking the city of Granada in southern Spain the Alhambra's gardens are seamlessly integrated into the palace architecture. The Patio de Los Leones or Court of Lions (left) contrasts with the shady, intimate courtyard with its large, central bowl fountain (below).

OPPOSITE Part of the Alhambra complex the detached Generalife was a summer retreat for the Nasrid rulers. This is the famous Patio de la Acequia (Court of the Water Channel).

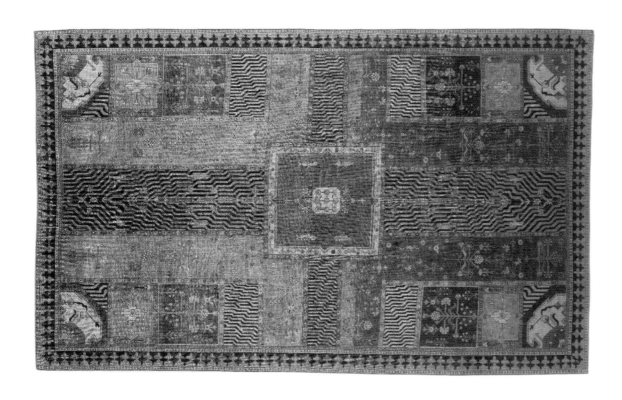

LEFT An eighteenth-century garden carpet made in north west Iran depicts a *chahar bagh* garden with flower beds surrounding the four rills that are fed by a central square pool.

BELOW Bagh-i Fin garden in Kashan, Iran is one of the nine gardens listed by UNESCO as a World Heritage Site under the name 'Persian Gardens'. It truly is a verdant and cool haven within a desert and famous for its blue-tiled watercourses.

OPPOSITE Two views of the Islamic garden made around the Ismaili Centre, Dubai show how adaptable, ingenious and relevant the *chahar bagh* model continues to be in contemporary Islamic garden-making.

Where space is limited the four beds may be paved with stone or tiles and the cool, ornamental surface strewn with carpets and cushions. But where space permits the beds are richly planted with flowers selected as much for their decorative as their aromatic qualities, for example jasmine, narcissi, violets, lilies and roses. The latter also became a popular theme in Islamic poetry. Trees which provided shade may include the 'acacias, palms and vines' mentioned in the Qur'an (2:268) as well as other symbolic species including cypress and plane. The former is symbolic of eternity and the latter is the tree of life. And as in *Jannah*, different kinds of fruit trees are also popular, especially fig, cherry, peach, citrus, pomegranate and almond. Those trees not present in this earthly expression are the four fabulous trees named in the Qu'ran: Zaqqûm, namely the Infernal Tree which grows in hell; the date palm of Sayyidatna Maryam (the Virgin Mary); the 'olive neither of the East nor West'; the Sidrat al-Muntahâ or Lote Tree of the Uttermost Boundary which becomes the Tree of Immortality in the Hadith literature.

Yet always the Islamic garden was and is more than simply a physical escape from the often harsh climate, an expression of a high art and a recreational space. In all its beauty it is also a refuge, blissful, delightful and eternal, a reminder of both the immanence and transcendence of God. Thus the earthly paradise garden is symbolic of the serenity and peace of heart and mind for which the soul yearns. At a profound level the garden is a private place, hidden away from the world and from people; a place for reflection, contemplation and nourishment of the 'Garden of the Heart'. Nowhere is this more discernible than in the use of water which is literally at the centre of the garden. 'Allah hath promised to Believers, men and women, gardens under which rivers flow, to dwell therein, and beautiful mansions in gardens of everlasting bliss' (9:72). On a literal and earthly plane this evokes the image of cooling water flowing through the garden but on a more profound level it suggests the cleansing and purifying of the spirit, the nurturing of the 'garden within'.

# Taj Mahal
## Agra, India

For two hundred years from the mid-sixteenth century Agra was the capital of the Mughal empire and here in 1528 the first emperor Babur created Ram Bagh, the prototype Mughal Islamic garden. Today the city is most famous for the white marble Taj Mahal. It was built by the fifth emperor Shah Jahan between 1632 and 1654 as the tomb of and memorial to his favourite wife Arjumand Banu Begam. In front of and below the building, which sits on a raised terrace on the edge of the River Yamuna, is a garden laid out in the classic *chahar bagh* or quadripartite form. However, given its significance, the garden form is more elaborate than a simple domestic garden. Here the four 'beds' are defined by a pair of main paths (*khiyaban*) which flank a shallow water canal (*nahr*), which themselves are watered by the centrally-positioned, raised, square white marble water tank (the *hauz*). Originally the four quadrants were further quartered and the beds planted with species brought from all over the Mughal empire and the air was heady with the perfume of their blooms. Sadly today the area is just grassy plats planted with trees.

Usually in such tomb gardens — for example the recently restored complex of Humayan, the second Mughal emperor in Delhi — the mausoleum is at the garden's centre, but this is not the case here if one only considers the garden and architecture complex that comprise the 'regular tourist experience'. However, an interesting recent discovery does in fact put the Taj Mahal in its proper place. For on the far bank and again below the beautiful building but aligned perfectly on it and of the correct proportions is the recently renovated Mehtab Bagh or 'Moon Lit Garden'. This garden is in fact more authentic than the more visited 'other half' and boasts an interesting feature. Deliberately positioned near to the river is a large, sunken octagonal pool. It is empty now, but when full would have reflected the mausoleum in its still waters. Imagine the view on a moonlit night of the white Taj reflected in the still, black waters of the pool. It may have been this striking image that gave rise to the rumours of the 'black Taj' — an exact copy of the white building, but this time in black marble and which was to be Shah Jehan's mausoleum.

BELOW LEFT A photograph from 1900 shows the garden in front of the Taj Mahal as far more richly planted than today and offers a more authentic impression of how the garden looked in its heyday.

BELOW RIGHT Viewed from the Great gate the extensive *chahar bagh* garden provides the perfect foreground to the mausoleum which in turn appears to float in the air.

ABOVE The reflection of the mausoleum in the River Yamuna gives an impression of how it would have appeared in the pool of the Mehtab Bagh.

BELOW The *nahr* flanked by a pair of *khiyaban* define the four large beds of the chahar bagh, which sadly today are simply lawn rather than further subdivided and richly planted.

OVERLEAF The Taj Mahal looking south from the northern shore of the River Yamuna and the location of the Mehtab Bagh.

# Renaissance

While the Islamic garden-making tradition has changed little since the eighth century the Italian Renaissance (which it is generally accepted began in earnest in the fifteenth century) signalled a paradigm shift in the Christian garden. The foundations of the Renaissance new world order had been laid in the preceding two centuries by the writings of Saint Thomas Aquinas (1225–74) and the scholar Petrarch (1304–74). Neither were iconoclastic, anti-Christian or even anti-clerical but both in their different ways reoriented man's perception of himself. There developed among scholars a consciousness that man was a rational and sentient being with the ability to think and decide for himself. Aquinas united Aristotelian logic and Christian doctrine into a syncretic intellectual system based on human experience and reason – natural theology – the application of which led to the examination and investigation of the nature of nature in order to understand the ordered, God-ordained cosmos. These studies in turn set in motion the scientific revolution. Petrarch on the other hand was the first Renaissance humanist. Within a Christian doctrinal matrix Petrarch initiated a new world view and method of open-ended enquiry in which human rather than divine matters assumed prime importance. This is in contrast with what humanism generally means today – a philosophical and ethical stance that emphasises the value and agency of human beings but which is typically aligned with secularism and with non-theistic religions.

Born out of a rediscovery of classical texts, natural theology and humanism the Italian Renaissance garden was a microcosm of the new world order and its form reflected the new spirit of enquiry as the small, introspective *hortus conclusus* gave way to an ordered, spacious and more outward-looking garden. And like their ancient Roman forebears so too rich Renaissance Romans and Florentines erected villas

in the country. Designed by Leon Battista Alberti and built between 1451 and 1457 for Giovanni de' Medici of the ruling Florentine dynasty, the Villa Medici at Fiesole is considered the prototype Renaissance villa in the *villa suburbana* version (as opposed to the defensive villa-castle form). It also boasts one of the earliest Italian Renaissance gardens. Inspired by Vitruvian formulae of symmetry and proportion and classical concepts of beauty, the garden is axially united with the villa and organised in a sequence of geometric divisions. Of course the Medici and other *nouveaux* patrician families created gardens to demonstrate their own power and magnificence and as set pieces for the enactment of elaborate

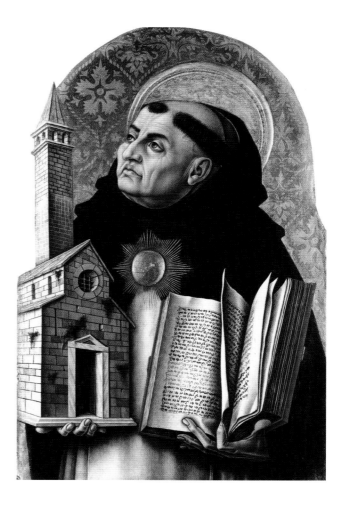

LEFT Painted on a wall in the Hall of the Fountain within the Villa d'Este, Tivoli this fresco by Girolamo Muziano shows the original layout of the garden.

RIGHT A panel of the large 'Demidoff Altarpiece' made for the high altar of San Domenico in Ascoli Piceno, Italy by Carlo Crivelli (1476) depicting St Thomas Aquinas, the foremost Renaissance proponent of natural theology.

and sumptuous ceremonials. At a deeper level though and while acknowledging that the real paradise of Eden had disappeared, the owners of these personal paradises – in line with the all-pervading spirit of inquiry – used them for the enjoyment of a new *otium* and gatherings of artists, philosophers and men of letters. For example, in 1469 Lorenzo il Magnifico inherited the Villa Medici following the premature death of his art-loving but debauched brother and moved his Platonic Academy into the villa. Thus the garden became a key location in which to investigate the interrelationship between God, man and nature.

It continued to be believed that God had fashioned both man and nature and that the divinely-created cosmos was both hierarchical and ordered. It was conjectured therefore that man could better understand God and his cosmic order by studying his relationship with this spiritual natural world which was also perceived as practical – a source of materials that met certain of man's needs, for example food, medicine, building materials, textiles and so on. Many aspects of this relationship were to be found in the garden which was essentially an ordered, man-made artistic expression fabricated from nature's raw materials. This was so not only in the design, ornament (statuary, grottoes, fountains et cetera) and planting but also in the physical construction thereof, the landscape itself, the land-forming and hydraulics, for

example. This garden-based interaction between human culture in the form of art and the divinely created natural world was subtle and complex, for when imitating nature both gardening and garden-making had not only to imitate its physical appearance but also its underlying divine order. Thus the distinction between art and nature was often deliberately blurred and became seen as what the humanist Jacopo Bonfadio termed in 1541 'una terza natura' or 'a third nature' in which nature and art fused into an indistinguishable and ordered whole but was neither the nor the other. For example, a garden grotto was an improved nature, simultaneously a classically-inspired work of art and an imitation of a naturally-occurring cave built from nature's materials.

During the High Renaissance of the sixteenth century gardens became larger, grander and more symmetrical, and filled with fountains, grottoes, water works and rare plants – especially sought-after were arrivals from the New World – and statues of ancient divinities, either excavated originals or newly sculpted. These pieces revived a classical imagery that, along with the new world view, superseded the Christian paradise imagery of the medieval *hortus conclusus*. Classical statuary and sculpture were widely used in elaborate programmes of allegory most often centred on the desired ancestry and attributes of the owner. For example, Cardinal Ippolito d'Este, creator of the eponymously-named villa in

The nineteenth-century engraving (left) by Ignazio Bonaiuti is of the Villa Medici at Fiesole. Designed by Leon Battista Alberti for Giovanni de' Medici and built between 1451 and 1457 it was the prototype Renaissance villa in the *villa suburbana* form. It also boasted one of the earliest Renaissance gardens but the original form is not known. Today, the garden (below) retains the 1772 conversion of the top terrace into an approach to the villa whilst the third terrace was redesigned by Cecil Pinsent and Geoffrey Scott between 1911 and 1923.

Tivoli (from 1550), repeatedly insinuated that his family was descended from Hercules.

In summary, the new Renaissance world view recognised the ordered, hierarchical cosmos created by God of which both man and nature were a part, and that the latter was a resource to be manipulated by the former. Reflecting the divine structure, the garden was intellectually a summation of contemporary knowledge of the natural world. Its physical form took on an ordered and structured layout containing all the variety of nature, but a nature fused with art — a third nature. As a microcosm that reflected the sacred macrocosm the garden became seen as a mechanism through which knowledge of the divine order could be deciphered.

OPPOSITE The Grotto at the Boboli Gardens, Florence is an example of *'una terza natura'* or 'a third nature' when the distinction between art and nature was deliberately blurred.

OVERLEAF The fine Renaissance gardens of the Giusti Palace in Verona, Italy.

# Villa d'Este
## Tivoli, Italy

Since antiquity the delightful hilltop town of Tibur (now Tivoli) some thirty kilometres east-north-east of Rome has had connotations as a sacred place. Here in the first century BCE the Temple of Vesta overlooked the spectacular waterfall on the Aniene river and was probably dedicated to one of the deities associated with the river. The Aniene was imbued with particular symbolism because it is a tributary of the Tiber and fed most of Rome's aqueducts in ancient times. Symbolically, the river was used to power — as it continues to do today — the garden's 500 jets.

Designed by Pirro Ligorio for Cardinal Ippolito II d'Este and begun in 1550 the four magnificent hectares of formal gardens command sweeping vistas out over the *campagna* as they cascade down the hillside behind the villa. But originally the visitor entered from the bottom of the garden and would have been awestruck by the first vista they encountered — straight along the main axis up to the villa above, and there, set on this main axis, was the dramatic Fountain of the Dragons. Supposedly built to honour the visit of Pope Gregory III in 1572 the fountain's main symbolism is in the dragon Ladon, and the educated visitor would immediately be asking himself, 'am I entering a contemporary Garden of the Hesperides?'

At the eastern end of the third terrace (from the top) is Rometta or the Fountains of Rome which depicts the ancient city well-watered and flourishing. This river symbolism is one of the religio-allegorical themes played out in the gardens of the Villa d'Este, the most spectacular and impressive of all High Renaissance gardens. At the western end of the third terrace the Oval Fountain (described soon after the garden's completion as the '*principalissima*' or finest in Italy) is overlooked by an enthroned statue of a local goddess known as the Tiburtine Sibyl. She also looks along the terrace and the Alley of the Hundred Fountains where water falling in three tiers represents the three tributaries that merge to form the Aniene.

OPPOSITE Water is a major symbolic theme within the gardens and no display is more spectacular that the multi-tiered Fountain of the Cascade.

RIGHT A bird's-eye perspective painting of the garden from an century engraving by Etienne Duperac. Note Rometta in the top right corner, the central Dragon Fountain and the Oval Fountain to the left.

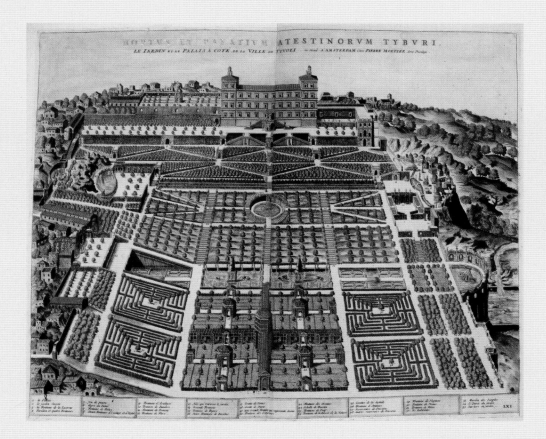

As a personal compensation for the cardinal, who had failed in his attempt to secure the papacy, the garden was also very much an example of power gardening. To demonstrate his and the d'Estes influence, wealth and lineage Ippolito ornamented his gardens with genuine classical statues which he had looted from the nearby ruins of Hadrian's Villa (it had been built by the emperor in the first half of the second century AD) and which celebrated his family's ancestry and its claim to be descended from Hercules himself.

ABOVE With Rometta in the foreground within the garden this view shows how the Italian Renaissance garden became outward looking and included vistas over the 'borrowed landscape' of the *campagna*.

RIGHT The superb Oval fountain

OPPOSITE Classical statuary and imagery is a thread that runs throughout the garden. The multi-breasted form of the Diana of Ephesus is symbolic of fertility.

# Elysium rediscovered

The influence of the Italian Renaissance and its gardens spread across Europe where their meaning and form were reinterpreted at a national level. At an artistic level the Renaissance evolved into the Baroque which in the garden reached its zenith at French Versailles (from 1664). There followed a century of imitation across Europe and by the turn of the eighteenth century English gardens had degenerated into pedantic repetitions of French and Dutch influenced ideas dominated by symmetry and geometry. In rejecting this stiff and autocratic garden form so often laid out with seemingly little thought given to scale or site there arose a new form of garden art that, while lacking any active religious symbolism, was strongly influenced by both the Renaissance view of nature and the belief system of ancient Greece. Neoclassicism once again popularised the architectural principles that had been rediscovered during the Renaissance while the Age of Enlightenment emphasised reason and individualism and, by challenging ideas set in tradition and faith, encouraged the advancement of knowledge through the scientific method.

Anthony Ashley-Cooper, 3rd Earl of Shaftesbury (1671–1713), who had been tutored by John Locke (the philosopher is thought to be one of the most influential Enlightenment thinkers), expressed the widely favoured opinion in his *Characteristics of Men, Manners, Opinions, Times, etc.* (1711) that landscapes had personalities. That is to say, as well as a physical form landscapes also have a metaphysical vital force that interacts with the human mind to stimulate emotions, moods and curiosity, elicit perceptions and form memories. To appreciate and understand this character of landscape – 'The Genius of the Place' – required a receptive and aware mind, one that would actively encounter stimulating landscapes and one which would analyse the experiences, the impressions and the imagination by means of rational thought.

Shaftesbury's assertion was one of a number of inspirations that aligned as the search for a new garden form turned towards a taste for nature and away from Baroque formality. Two more were to be found on the library shelves and walls of so many country houses. Just as classical works had influenced the Renaissance, so again the texts of Homer, Virgil, Pliny (both the Younger and Elder) and others resonated with those desiring a pastoral idyll. As too did the classically-inspired landscape paintings of Claude Lorrain (1600–82) and Nicolas Poussin (1594–1665) depicting verdant and sylvan scenes peppered with classical architecture and ruins. A third formative influence was the Grand Tour undertaken by wealthy young gentlemen as part of their education. These impressionable, sensate minds were exposed to the dramatic landscapes of Europe during the journey to Italy

RIGHT Anthony Ashley Cooper, 3rd Earl of Shaftesbury popularised the notion that the natural landscape has a vital force to which the human mind responds.

RIGHT Paintings of classically-inspired scenes set within a stylised nature such as Nicolas Poussin's *Landscape with Antique Tomb and Two Figures* (c.1642–47) had a significant impact on the emergence of the English Landscape Garden.

BELOW The Grand Tour, on which young gentlemen experienced the dramatic landscapes of Europe on their way to Rome where they revelled in the classical ruins, also had a significant influence. This is *Goethe visiting the Colosseum in Rome* by Jacob-Philippe Hackert (c.1790).

Three English landscapes on which William Kent worked.

Today the landscape at Rousham, Oxfordshire (left) is the most unaltered of Kent's classically-inspired picturesque landscapes. The *View from the Cascade Terrace, Chiswick* by George Lambert (below) also shows Chiswick House, London which was one of the earliest expressions of Palladian-revival architecture. Arguably Kent's masterpiece was the allegorically-laden landscape at Stowe, Buckinghamshire (opposite). Here in the Elysian Fields the Temple of Ancient Virtue is reflected in the River Styx.

OVERLEAF The photograph overleaf is of a triple-arched bridge at Stowe.

and, once there, experienced genuine classical ruins and the Renaissance gardens now under a gentle patina of age.

The mental associations and impressions of all three influences melded together with new Enlightenment thinking to foster the English landscape garden. This new style of landscape-making underwent an evolutionary process lasting the best part of a century but the influence of classical writings and ancient Grecian groves and temples on this garden form is most evident in the picturesque designs of William Kent (1685–1748) who spent nineteen years training as a painter, ten of them in Rome. Kent applied a painterly eye to his three-dimensional canvases and devised pieces of garden theatre in which the designed landscape became a living picture, a work of art set within a tamed, idealised and sculptured nature. Using the ha-ha to bring into the frame views and vistas from 'borrowed nature', Kent arranged sinuous paths, serpentine lakes, soft lawns planted with groves of trees interspersed with distant prospects and studded with temples and statuary. These picturesque scenes, so full of allegory and literary and emotional overtones that stimulated the imagination and evoked moods of tranquillity, gaiety, grandeur and melancholy, were not English in their inspiration but took their lead from romantic images of classical Greece and Rome. Yet in a very Renaissance way these landscapes were simultaneously another incarnation of the third nature.

# Eastern religions

There are fundamental differences in the way that Western and Eastern religions define the relationship between God, man and nature. As we have seen, the Ancient Greeks (and as far as we know, the Minoans too) had a nature-centric religion. They populated the natural earthly world with their gods and worshipped them in sacred places to celebrate or placate the divine-derived forces of nature. Judaeo-Christian religions, while believing in a divinely-created and ordered cosmos, place man above nature. And while their god occasionally visited this world (for example Eden) he is also believed to inhabit an other-worldly place. When we turn our focus East, however, we find a series of belief systems that are distinctly nature-oriented but in which nature is perceived as the product of powerful, non-theistic forces or energies. These doctrines, some of which coexisted alongside one another and experienced levels of syncretism, do not elevate man above nature but see him as an intrinsic and equal component. As a result Eastern religions manifest a more direct bond between people and nature than their Western counterparts.

To grasp basic Eastern cosmology Western readers must also understand both the fundamental differences in the way we perceive time and the way Judaic, Christian and Islamic religions construe human life. Broadly speaking, Western cultures see life as a unique event — we are born, we live, and we die; this life event occurring within a timeframe conceptualised as linear. A succession of unique happenings make history a forward-moving drama in which Western religions have devised creation myths to explain that the universe came into being as the result of a unique, divine act. In the East it is widely held by the devout that the cosmos was/is created by natural forces and has always existed and thus that time is cyclical and repetitive, undergoing vast cycles of evolution and decline lasting for millions of years. History is

therefore also comprehended as a series of potentially infinite cycles which may vary hugely in length of time and within which similar patterns of events recur with no fixed goal or purpose. For example, the cycle of the seasons and nature in general is one of birth, growth, death … and renewal. Thus to the Eastern mind, which understands man is an integral (and equal) part of nature and the universe, it was not strange to presume that human existence follows a similar pattern and passes through an extended cycle of births and deaths.

LEFT A dramatic landscape painting by Southern Song dynasty artist Ma Yuan shows the stylised mix of nature and human activity so central to the Chinese approach to nature.

ABOVE This Tibetan watercolour on cotton of a mandala contains a representation of a garden (in green) populated with figures and located outside the red square walled enclosure within which are set four gates.

# Ancient China

The three major religio-philosophical doctrines that shaped both the Chinese belief system and garden — Taoism (Daoism), Confucianism and Buddhism — developed or were introduced and became established during early Chinese dynastic history. And they all evolved within an existing and extensive mythology associated with agriculture. The first five mythological farming emperors were variously credited with learning the secrets of animal husbandry and beasts of burden, tools and implements, the domestication of plants and cultivation techniques (including soil improvement and irrigation), as well as the control of fire and cooking. From the earliest times, therefore, the Chinese approached nature as a resource to be utilised, but in a respectful way that Maggie Keswick termed 'harmonious adjustment', regarding the 'alteration of their environment as adornment rather than subjugation'. That is to say nature's plenitude was realised and its beauty tempered while being esteemed and revered as part of the larger and holistic natural universe of which man was also an integral and equal partner. For a comprehensive and broad history of the Chinese garden the reader is referred to Keswick's authoritative *The Chinese Garden*.

The Yellow River which empties into the Bohai Sea to the south east of modern-day Beijing is said to be the cradle of Chinese civilisation, which itself dates to the second

millennium BCE. The nation's written history begins in the Shang dynasty (c.1700–1046 BCE) at a time when in the West the Minoans were at their zenith, in ancient Egypt the New Kingdom came to power (1550–1069 BCE) and the Assyrian kings were in control of Mesopotamia. The subsequent and long-lasting Zhou dynasty (1045–256 BCE) saw territorial expansions into the Yangtze River valley and the first of many population migrations from north to south that have peppered Chinese history.

However, from the eighth century BCE the kingdom began to fragment and localise into hundreds of small states. Instability was increased by invasions from the north west including those by the Qin. In spite of this disruption the Zhou dynasty was also marked by substantial cultural, literary and philosophical advances. Of fundamental significance were the works of Confucius (551–479 BCE) and the emergence of Taoism; and in line with the religio-reverence for nature princes made the earliest forms of designed landscapes – ornamental hunting parks.

# Confucianism

Confucius was among other things a politician and philosopher and his teachings were subsequently developed into a system known collectively as Confucianism, a set of virtue ethics that operate both within a socio-political framework and at a personal level. Confucianism was elevated to the official imperial state philosophy by the Emperor Wu of Han (Liu Che r.141–87 BCE), and in AD 140 Confucius's texts – the Five Classics – became required reading for those taking civil service examinations, a practice that continued nearly unbroken until the end of the nineteenth century.

Confucius, living and working in a time of conflict, idealised the quasi-Golden Age rural idyll of the mythical farming emperors and advocated a balanced mix of simplicity and refinement. Firmly believing that farming should be the basis of the state, Confucius melded bucolicism with promotion of ritual and the 'superior man'. The latter was achieved by adherence to and practice of self-cultivation focusing on sincerity, virtue and knowledge, the development of moral

LEFT Fog wreaths a landscape of mountains and rice terraces at Longsheng near the town of Guilin, Guangxi province. Man's activities both make use of nature's bounty while simultaneously and sympathetically complementing the natural beauty of the scene.

RIGHT A statue of that most influential of politician-philosophers Confucius erected within a Confucian temple in Shanghai.

perfection, and the attainment and application of skilled judgement over strict obedience to explicit rules of behaviour. This in essence is a Chinese expression of humanism (in the modern meaning of the word) blended with a this-worldly awareness of certain cosmological and metaphysical elements of the *tian* (*tian* has a complex meaning but evolved to signify at the same time a single omnipotent deity and heaven, and is analogous with the Tao of Taoism. Within this framework the garden became a setting in which the scholarly, self-improved man was able to express his learning and sophistication by emulating refinement and simplicity.

Perhaps the most famous of all Confucian gardens was made during the Song dynasty (AD 960–1279) by the retired politician-scholar-gardener, the poet and historian Sima Guang (1021–1086). *Du Le Yuan* (The Garden of Solitary Enjoyment) was in fact an urban garden within the city of Luoyang (now in western Henan province), where Sima Guang tried to create a rustic simplicity in about 1.5 hectares. It contained a fish pond in the shape of a tiger's paw with a lake in the centre boasting a picturesque fisherman's hut made by tying together the tops of a circle of bamboo likened to a jade ring. The key building was the Pavilion of Study, home to his library of 5000 volumes and Sima Guang could see the distant mountains from a small room built on a terrace.

Writing in the third person Sima Guang describes his Confucian use of his garden in 'Record of the Garden of

ABOVE The Pavilion of Study garden created by Sima Guang within his famous Confucian garden which he named the 'Park of Solitary Enjoyment'.

# Taoism

With its misty origins in indigenous shamanism and animism Taoism is a religious-philosophical-ethical tradition. Its formalisation is often associated with Laozi (Lao Tzu) the purported author of *Tao Te Ching (Taode jing)* sometime in the third or fourth century BCE. This philosophical and political text focuses on the Tao (meaning 'way' or 'path') as the proper guiding principle for personal behaviour and for leading others. The Tao is also explained as a primal force that existed 'before Heaven and Earth' and from which all forms emerged. Thus Chinese Taoism doctrine holds nature to have been created by a spiritual energy or transcendental force that pervades the universe and is possessed by all phenomena. This force is the *Ch'i (qi)* or breath. Taoism places an especial emphasis on reverence of nature and within nature on man's relationship with the universe. A particular aim is to create and maintain harmony within the universe, something that may be achieved at least in part by personal behaviour including *wu wei* (effortless effort, or action through inaction), vitality and longevity.

Solitary Enjoyment' which was included within the *Sima Wen Gong Wen Ji* (The collected works of Sima Guang). The following translation was made by Paul Clifford and appears in Keswick's *The Chinese Garden*:

> He usually spent a lot of time reading in the hall. He took the sages as his teachers and the many virtuous men (of antiquity) as his friends, and he got an insight into the origins of benevolence and righteousness, and investigated the ins and outs of the Rites and of Music….The principles of things gathered before his eyes. If his resolve was weary and his body exhausted, he took a rod and caught fish, he held up his sleeves and picked herbs, made a breach in the canal and watered the flowers, took up an axe and cut down bamboos, washed his hands in the water to cool himself down, and, near the highest spot, let his eyes wander to and fro wherever he pleased. Occasionally, when a bright moon came round and a clear wind arrived, he walked without any restrictions. His eyes, his lungs, his feelings were all his very own….What enjoyment could replace this? Because of this he called the garden the Park of Solitary Enjoyment.

A later, eighteenth-century example of rusticity (perhaps somewhat incongruously) set within a religio-landscape was the working farm made on Longevity Hill within the Summer Palace near Beijing by the Qianlong Emperor.

Another ancient tradition — evidence for early forms of which date to as early as the fifth millennium BCE — that exerted an influence on garden design is geomancy and specifically *feng-shui* (literally 'wind-water'). *Feng-shui* is incorporated within Taoist belief but not exclusive to it and is not easily comprehended by the Western mind. For a succinct analysis of the subject the reader is referred to Günter Nitschke's excellent *Japanese Gardens*. In essence though, *feng-shui* is a traditional form of Chinese natural science that takes as a starting point an holistic and naturalistic view of the cosmos in which man is perceived as an integral part of nature and its energy fields. Psychosomatic welfare is created by applying the most favourable design and location of human structures (a garden, house, grave, city et cetera) within the natural or man-made environment according to geophysical factors (topography, geography, magnetic fields and so on) and astral phenomena (star movements, lunar phases and so on) which are divined through an amalgam of cosmological rules (the geomantic compass) and intuitive cognition. Two aspects of *feng-shui* that were also of particular relevance to Taoism and the Chinese garden were both the *Ch'i* and the reciprocal polarity expressed through the *yin-yang* dualism. In essence *yin* and *yang* are complementary and interdependent forces (for example dark and light) that interact to form a dynamic system in which the whole is greater than the assembled parts.

The mythology of the Immortals is also a strong component within Taoism. The legendary eight Immortals or *xian* were not gods but enchanted, perfect human beings who had sought and achieved immortality. They were believed to inhabit lofty palaces perched among the peaks of the mythical Mount Kunlun (the Himalaya) far to the west and the Isles of the Blessed (known too as the Isles of the Immortals and the Mystic Isles) far out in the eastern sea.

The Isles were also believed to have wonderful high mountains as well as deep misty valleys and blue rushing rivers. Here, where beautiful pavilions lined the seashore, the Immortals lived in perfect harmony enjoying a verdant paradise graced with the most exotic fauna and flora, including life-prolonging trees and immortality-bestowing fungi. It was believed that to reach these elusive islands would confer

immortality and they were actively sought out by various emperors who dispatched a succession of unsuccessful expeditions. And, within a belief system that revered nature, mountains both real and mythological became especially esteemed for the beauty of their often spectacular scenery and their mythological association. This reverence, we shall see, found expression within the garden.

Ending the Warring States period (461–221 BCE) the Qin king Ying Zheng united the various kingdoms to create the first Chinese empire and, calling himself Qin Shi Huang, was ruler of the Qin dynasty from 220 BCE until his death in 210. This first emperor began building the Great Wall and had the Terracotta Army constructed for his tomb. He also continued the Zhou fashion for making ornamental hunting parks and had the remarkable Shanglin park built between the Wei River and the Zhongnan Mountain to the south of the capital Chang'an (now Xi'an, the capital of Shaanxi province).

LEFT This painting by an unknown artist demonstrates the popularity of mountains as a subject. Moreover the white and black echoes the dualism that was a cornerstone of so much religio-philosophical thought central to Chinese garden design.

RIGHT In this scene by Qiu Ying dating to the sixteenth century and the Ming dynasty the beautiful mountains are central to the composition which depicts the peach garden in the blissful land of the Immortals.

Encircled by stout walls, like the empire itself, this huge park peppered with palaces and pavilions was laid out with mountains and valleys, rivers, lakes and islands, forests and open spaces to provide a habitat for hordes of game. It was more than just an imperial pleasure ground and hunting park, and in many ways and in a single place it shared and fulfilled many of the same purposes as an Achaemenid *pairidaēza*, and more. Shanglin was intended to reflect the supremacy, wealth and magnificence of the emperor while the hunt itself was a display of prestige and military force that reminded visiting dignitaries to remain submissive and loyal. As a microcosm in which so many natural riches might be found the park was filled with a botanical and zoological collection that reflected the diversity and wealth of the newly-united China. Moreover the park also provided a symbolic setting for those religio-ceremonials performed by the emperor that ritualistically emphasised the bond between man, the universe and the supernatural. Such ritual activities were important because it was believed that the emperor, the Son of Heaven, acted as a conduit to earth for the power or forces of which the cosmos was composed. And just as the world seemed to

revolve celestially around Polaris (called in Chinese texts the 'Great Heavenly Emperor'), so earthly state and religious affairs revolved around the emperor. Both star and man were a form of *axis mundi* and since Polaris is aligned almost due north, so a northerly alignment became associated with the emperor and thus an auspicious geomantic aspect.

In the aftermath of another civil war following Qin Shi Huang's death, the short-lived Qin dynasty was replaced by the Han dynasty (202 BCE – AD 220). Founded by Emperor Gao (r. 202–195 BCE) it marked a long period of stability and prosperity that consolidated China as a unified state under a central imperial bureaucracy and saw territorial gains extend the empire to what is basically China today. Emphasising stability and order in a well-structured society Confucianism became the state-endorsed orthodoxy and shaped culture, science and the arts. Alongside Confucianism, Taoism became an organised religion in the second century AD with the founding of the Tianshi (Celestial Masters) sect by Zhang Daoling. Taoist mystical notions of immortality and paradise were expressed in the basic garden elements of rock and water – *shan* meaning mountain and *shui* meaning water

LEFT *The Shanglin Park: Imperial Hunt* is another painting by Qiu Ying, this time depicting a real rather than a mythological subject. Such naturalistic but man-made landscape also gave the emperor an opportunity to display his power and perform his sacro-religious role.

BELOW In this depiction of Penglai Island the artist Yuan Jiang (active 1680–1730) attempts to capture the essence of this, one of the three paradisiacal islands inhabited by the Immortals.

and together *shan-shui* means landscape. The phrase also encapsulates but wholly loses in translation the most important metaphysical concepts inspiring the formal language of Chinese (and, later, Japanese) garden design and landscape painting – the duality of mountain and water. Thus, too, the beautiful, delightful, sea-girt Isles of the Blessed and dramatic, towering mountain scenery of the Immortals also became a favourite subject for poetry and the decorative arts and established the paradisiacal theme that runs throughout Chinese garden making.

In a wonderfully optimistic display of reverse logic Emperor Wu of Han (r. 141–87 BCE) decided not to pursue the Immortals but rather entice them to visit him. Thus within the Shanglin garden he built the Qianzhang (Jianzhang) palace and made a paradise garden associated with it. From the large Lake of Primary Liquid rose three substantial islands named Penglai, Fangzhang and Yingzhou. As well as sharing their name they resembled as closely as imagined those mythical isles rising from the seas, and were planted with remarkable plants. The same names were given to three mountains built in the garden, where too suitably potent palaces were erected for his anticipated guests, and on the shores of the lake the emperor had constructed a sixty-one metre (200-feet) tall platform from which he would communicate with the Immortals.

Even though the desired guests never showed this garden became a huge inspiration for Chinese garden-makers, and a few centuries later Emperor Yang of Sui (r. AD 604–18) attempted to outdo it. As part of his new, second and eastern capital of Luoyang he had a landscape park made with a circumference of 121 kilometres (75 miles). Using a labour force of a million Sui Yangdi had a ten-kilometre (6-mile) long lake dug and from it rose three islands on which stood beautiful pavilions. Further lakes and streams symbolised the five lakes and four seas of the ordered universe and provided access to the sixteen water pavilions each with their own delightful gardens, whilst the park itself was filled with rare and unusual flora and fauna. How much piety Sui Yangdi was attempting to achieve with displays of such magnificence and extravagance is debatable. More certainly the park was an expression of the emperor's megalomania and a part cause of his eventual murder.

# Buddhism

Taoist garden iconography coexisted alongside influences derived from the teachings of Confucianism and, later, Buddhism. Recent research indicates that Buddhism was introduced to China from the Indian subcontinent during the reign of Emperor Wu who ruthlessly suppressed it. Nevertheless Buddhism was widely established by the third century AD. In most Buddhist traditions Siddhārtha Gautama (c.563–483 BCE or, alternatively, c.480–400 BCE) is regarded as the Supreme Buddha ('awakened' or 'enlightened one') of our age. He was born a prince of the Sakya tribe of Nepal to Queen Māyā who, according to tradition, gave birth under a sal tree (*Shorea robusta*) in a garden in Lumbini. As the tree magically bent down to her and she grasped a branch, so the Buddha emerged from her right side. Aged twenty-nine Siddhārtha renounced the comforts of his privileged life in order to seek the meaning of the worldly suffering he saw around him. Six years of yoga and deprivation left him none the wiser and so he embarked on a regime of meditation,

developing his own middle way or path of moderation that avoided the extremes of self-indulgence and self-mortification. Vowing not to arise until he had found the truth Siddhārtha famously sat beneath a pipal tree (*Ficus religiosa*) in Bodh Gaya, India. Forty-nine days of meditation later, during the full moon of May and with the morning star rising, Siddhārtha achieved enlightenment and became the Buddha. The tree became the Bodhi tree and its descendant still grows in the temple complex at Bodh Gaya, part of the Mahabodhi temple complex in the state of Bihar.

Buddhists believe that they are reborn into one of six realms – Hell, Ghosts, Animals, *Asuras*, Human or Heaven, the destination dependent on the individual's karma. Karma

BELOW LEFT A brass sculpture from the Nepalese School depicting the Queen Māyā giving birth to the Buddha beneath a sal tree.

BELOW RIGHT An ancient sandstone carving on the wall of the ninth-century Borobudur temple in Yogyakarta, Indonesia of a group of Buddhist worshippers under a Bodhi tree.

ABOVE A silk cosmological mandala of the Yuan dynasty (1271–1368) with Mount Meru at its centre.

BELOW The striking red and unusually shaped flower of the sal or cannonball tree.

# Pure Land Buddhism

Buddhism shares with Taoism a quiet meditative practice as a means toward spiritual awareness, and a part of the assimilation process of Buddhism in China was a level of concept-matching (akin to early Christians adopting pagan celebrations) that saw Buddhism adapt the Taoist attitude to nature. Thus the main impact of Buddhism on the religio-symbolism of Chinese garden-making was that nature imagery intensified and new meanings were added to existing ideas and motifs, particularly from its nature-centric approach and mountain reverence into which the concept of Mount Meru was melded. There was too a level of syncretism with a particular Buddhist sect, that of Pure Land. This devotional sect originated in the Gandhara region of what is now northern Pakistan and eastern Afghanistan and reached China as early as AD 147. With its focus on Amitābha Buddha it teaches that it is possible to be reborn painlessly through the flowers of the lotus (*Nelumbo speciosum*) into the Pure Land, which is described in the *Infinite Life Sutra* as a land of beauty that surpasses all other realms. Once reborn here the cycle was ended and thus the individual had, in effect, achieved enlightenment and now dwelt permanently in a paradisiacal landscape. This landscape of mountain ranges separated by oceans not only mirrored the magic dwellings of the Immortals but in its own right had a particular impact on Japanese gardens as we shall subsequently discover.

was defined by the Buddha by reference to moral choices and the acts consequent upon them, and an agricultural metaphor is frequently used. Karma is likened to sowing seeds. Some are good and at some point in the future will produce sweet fruits, others are bad and will bear bitter fruits. Thus the karmic choices we make today will at some future point (in this or a subsequent life) mature as good or bad deeds. Of the six realms Heaven, which mythology locates above the great Mount Meru that lies at the centre of the world (as the *axis mundi*) is the residence of the gods (*deva*), those beings who have accumulated sufficient good karma to justify a rebirth in paradise. Nevertheless, bar the paradisiacal environment Buddhism grants no special privileges to those who have a heavenly rebirth. *Deva* do not create the cosmos or control human destiny, they cannot forgive sins nor pass judgement on human beings, nor is heaven a place of permanent salvation. Like all humans the *deva* are subject to karmic law and will be reborn in a lower realm when their good *karma* expires.

# Scholar gardens

In the centuries following the collapse of the Han dynasty the general malaise brought on by political weakness and hypocrisy, clan wars and the terror of invaders from the north resulted in a loss of faith in Confucianism. How could such an ethical system have led China to such disaster and confusion? New answers were sought in alternative philosophies and the soteriological doctrines of Taoism and Buddhism came to dominate intellectual life. Many of the elite made another of the mass southerly migrations to wild and beautiful lands which by their standards were barely civilised. Here a second imperial centre was established south of the Yangtze River at Jiankang (near present-day Nanjing in Jiangsu province).

By the third century AD private villa gardens (as opposed to imperial palace gardens) made by discerning Chinese scholars began to develop. They were based on an admixture of two different but interlinked motifs that became a constant for the next 1500 years – the matrix of nature mythology and religio-philosophy promulgated by Taoism, Buddhism and Confucianism, and the intimately connected arts of landscape painting, poetry, music and calligraphy. Such gardens were made by mandarins – high officials within the nine ranks of the imperial bureaucracy (and thus recipients of imperial favour) and for whom a thorough understanding of Confucianism had been a prerequisite for their professional life. When the winds of political change blew cold and they found themselves out of favour many such wealthy gentleman scholars, now with the time and means, engaged in a refined

retirement, a Chinese form of *otium*. Such scholars were expected to be not only connoisseurs but also practitioners of the above arts and of course, garden design.

Here Confucianism with its emphasis on self-improvement continued to be a guiding light, as did Taoism, Buddhism and wilderness travel. One aspect in which Buddhism differed from Taoism was in its establishment of remote mountain monasteries where, rather than indulging in Taoist hermitic meditative practices, groups of monks sought enlightenment

OPPOSITE A fifteenth-century Tibetan painting on cotton of the Amitābha (or Jina) Buddha of Infinite Light sat in the midst of His Pure Land paradise.

ABOVE The staggeringly beautiful Lu Shan mountains in Jiangxi province, sometimes named as the fabled home of the Immortals and a great inspiration for Chinese garden-makers (see p.110).

RIGHT Situated in the hills on the outskirts of modern-day Xi'an, Wangchuan villa was the rural retreat of poet, musician and landscape painter Wang Wei (699–761). Renowned for its spectacular scenery here Wei made one of the most famous gardens of ancient China.

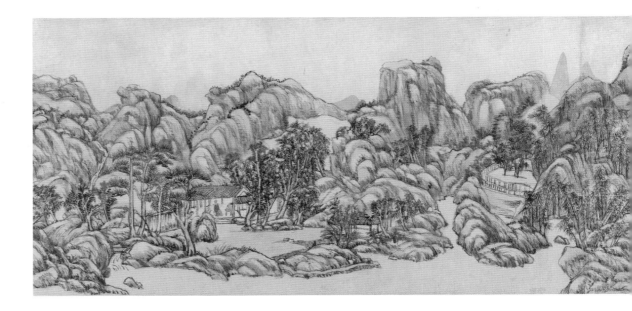

together. In such community-based monasteries built amongst picturesque peaks the monks were often joined by scholars and artists. Thus was reinforced the Chinese proclivity for wilderness and the desire to achieve spiritual fulfilment in, and complete human integration with, nature. The famous monastery founded by the Buddhist monk Hui-yuan (c. AD 334–416) a follower of Pure Land Buddhism, among the extraordinarily beautiful Lu Shan mountain range (to the south of Jiujiang City in Jiangxi province) became a particularly sought-after destination and a major inspiration for landscape painting and gardens.

Scholar gardens were very much an expression of a (Confucian-improved) self which expressed the owner's character, life and pursuits as well as their intellectual, metaphysical and philosophical thinking. In their design and composition the gardens therefore contained symbolically representative features, made provision for intellectual pursuits and offered opportunities for amusement. Here the owner would meditate in solitude, study and practice the arts, and use the garden for recreation – family gatherings, boating trips, musical and poetry recitals, entertaining guests and drinking. The latter was either done quietly alone or in

company and sometimes involved a delightful and unusual drinking game. Some gardens boast a poetry pavilion, for example the Pavilion of Bestowing Wine (*Xi Shang Tang*) within the Qianlong garden inside the Forbidden City in Beijing. Set in the floor is a sinuous rill, a cup-floating stream. Upstream a cup of wine would be floated on the water and guests had to compose a poem by the time the cup had bobbed its course. This tradition began at the Orchid pavilion near present-day Shaoxing in Zhejiang province and was celebrated in a famous calligraphy scroll by Wang Xizhi (AD 353).

As the Chinese garden developed down the centuries, its conventions became established and its mature form appeared in the Southern Song dynasty (1127–1279). Spectacular examples were made in and around the new capital Hangzhou in Zhejiang province (the north of the country having again been invaded and conquered) where, were it needed, the surrounding landscape of lakes and hills itself provided added inspiration. A survivor which retains distant echoes of its former detailed and complex self is the still beautiful *Xi Hu* (West Lake).

Many of the private gardens of the capital of the silk trade, Suzhou in Jiangsu province, which were made from the

OPPOSITE The Orchid pavilion in the Lanzhu mountain near Shaoxing where timed poetry composition began.

RIGHT AND BELOW An example in Suzhou of a scholar's garden. The Humble Administrator's garden which was originally made by Lu Guimeng, a Tang dynasty scholar. Its name was inspired by verse of Pan Yue's Idler's Prose: 'I enjoy a carefree life by planting trees and building my own house ... I irrigate my garden and grow vegetables for me to eat ... such a life suits a retired official like me well.' This verse symbolised Wang's desire to retire from politics and adopt a simple life.

eleventh century onward, for example, *Wang Shi Yuan* (the Master-of-the-Nets Garden), *Zhuozheng Yuan* (the Humble Administrator's Garden) and *Liú Yuán* (the Lingering Garden) have fared better. Nevertheless most underwent modification in later centuries and extensive restoration in the twentieth.

Given the very personal, Confucian nature of the scholar gardens' creators it is not possible to make generalisations concerning the specifics of their individual designs. However all contained certain symbolic elements and it is possible to examine the garden as an outward and visible expression of *Ch'i*. As already identified, two essential elements were *shan* (mountain) and *shui* (water). The bright, hard and upright male *yang* of rocky islands and mountains and the duality of the feminine *yin* of wet, receptive and dark water also chimed with Taoist nature reverence and Immortal mythology. And as well as a religious and geomantic relevance water and rock had symbolic associations with the reverence for natural landscapes, perhaps encountered during wilderness travel or depicted on a favourite landscape painting. Moreover such

garden elements provided a contemplative element, a rock could represent a single mountain or a whole mountain range and now miniaturised in the garden offered the opportunity to meditate over their beauty and symbolic associations.

Buildings and plants were the gardens' other two major components. It may seem strange to Western readers who so avidly fill their gardens with floral riches from China that Chinese garden-makers did not. Even stranger perhaps given that the garden was intended to be a microcosm of nature and China is possessed of a particularly rich and beautiful native flora. This is not to say that plants were not considered important – they were, and they generated an extensive literature. From the fourteenth century onward and in conjunction with the developing mood of conservatism the taxa cultivated became increasingly restricted to those with traditional affiliations – those symbolic of ideas, moral qualities and emotional states, for example, together with those possessed of specific associations, for instance with particular deities, Buddhist saints and Taoist Immortals. And of course plants

OPPOSITE AND ABOVE Albeit now diminished Xi Hu or West Lake is a survivor of the beautiful gardens created during the Southern Song dynasty around the new capital of Hangzhou in Zhejiang province. Note the lotus growing in the lake.

OVERLEAF An ancient Chinese rock garden in Suzhou.

were revered for their seasonal changes, symbolic of the cyclical pattern of nature and time.

There is insufficient space here to record all such symbolic plants but two examples highlight the complexity of these associations and symbolisms. The *sui han san yu* or Three Friends of Winter (the term dates to the thirteenth-century writings of Lin Ching-hsi) refer to the pine, bamboo and plum (*Prunus mume* is also somewhat confusingly known as the Japanese apricot) which are revered because when all other plants are dormant they display vitality. Together they became a symbol of determination and perseverance in the face of adversity, providing inspiration through consolation and determination. Individually the sturdy, gnarled and craggy pine represents strength and virtue to overcome all. The evergreen bamboo with its hollow canes represents stamina, tolerance and open-mindedness and its flexibility and strength are a symbol of cultivation and integrity through which one yields but does not break (just as would the consummate Confucian gentleman). The winter- flowering plum brings a beautiful elegance during this desolate season and symbolises inner beauty and humble display under adverse conditions. Perhaps the most symbolic of all garden plants, though, is the lotus, Hui Lin Li in his *Garden Flowers of China* offers this translation of the poem *Ai lian shuo* ('On the love of the lotus') by the famous scholar, Zhou Dunyi (1017–73):

It emerges from muddy dirt but is not contaminated; it reposes modestly above the clear water; hollow inside and straight outside, its stems do not straggle or branch. Its subtle perfume pervades the air far and wide. Resting there with its radiant purity, the lotus is something to be appreciated from a distance, not profaned by intimate approach.

Confucianists saw it as a model for the Superior Man, it was the emblem of He Xiangu, one of the eight Immortals and thus a popular Taoist symbol, and long before its arrival in China Buddhism had a deep association with the lotus. The Buddha is frequently depicted seated on the flower's open petals and the plant is used as a metaphor. Growing up from the muddy bottom of a lake and putting forth such delightful blooms was analogous to the soul struggling up from the slime of the material world, through emotions (the water) and finding enlightenment in the ether above. And finally, when spoken, the Chinese name for lotus sounds not dissimilar to the word for harmony and thus the plant is often used as a symbol for friendship, peace and happy union.

Buildings — halls and pavilions (*tings*) connected by paths, bridges, galleries and winding corridors (*lang*) — create the garden framework as well as providing locations where the scholar could perform his various studies and activities. But to Western eyes the plan of a scholar garden produces much the same effect as visiting one — mild perplexity and disorientation. A sense of infinite extension and mysterious distance is in part achieved by concealing the definite boundary and extent of the garden so that there is a sense of endless succession and expansion, of unlimited time and space. Yet within the space the many and varied garden elements, experiences and meanings are densely packed together and with seemingly no discernible or rhythmic order to their arrangement. Some were traditional symbolic associations that would have been obvious to the educated visitor, for, as Jean Cooper notes, the scholar Zhang Zhao (AD 156–236) poetically observed that:

> Planting flowers serves to invite butterflies, piling up rocks serves to invite the clouds, planting pine trees serves to invite the wind . . . planting banana trees serves to invite the rain and planting willow trees serves to invite the cicada.

第九一年都市王

第二七日初江王

第八百日平正王

第三七日宗帝王

第六七日變成王

南无道明和尚

南无金毛師子

第五七日閻羅王

宗　　　王　　　道判官

But in another important way this cramming is very deliberate because as a microcosm of nature's plenitude the garden had to symbolise aesthetically the entire universe. Of course the space cannot contain *all* the universe but the constantly changing vistas and the emotions that they stir is a result of the constant and restless fluctuation between the opposites of the *yin-yang* dualisms: the solid and the void, valleys and mountains, waters and sky, sunshine and shadow, height and depth, heat and cold and so on. Nevertheless, as Keswick explains, this ceaseless alternation, for example the fluid, ever-changing *yin* of water and the rigid and stable *yang* mountains (rocks) cannot be totally accounted for in aesthetic terms, and, countering various suggestions to the contrary, convincingly argues that there was no deliberate symbolism involved in the overall garden design. Rather, the connection between the aesthetic and the symbolic was eruditely summarised by the eighteenth-century writer Shen Fu in his autobiography *Six Records of a Floating Life*:

In laying out garden pavilions and towers, suites of rooms and covered walkways, piling up rocks into mountains, or planting flowers to form a desired shape, the aim is to see the small in the large, to see the large in the small, to see the real in the illusory and to see the illusory in the real….Sometimes you conceal, sometimes you reveal, sometimes you work on the surface, sometimes in depth.

Thus the garden was more than simply a physical simulation of sacred scenery. It was also intended to stimulate a connection and unity with the universe. For example, standing in a snow-blanketed garden oblivious of the cold and focused on a billow of plum blossom the viewer vigorously and spontaneously feels his/her heart flowering in unity with the tree and thus through the garden experiences the mysterious workings of the Tao. Similarly a microcosm of the Tao within the microcosm of the universe that was the garden were the *taihu shi* or fantastically-shaped, water-eroded limestone monoliths which were avidly collected during the Song dynasty. Especially sought-after were the 'scholar rocks' from Lake Tai located west of Suzhou. To quote Keswick again:

The stones, billowing out from narrow bases, hollowed by weather and time, pitted with holes and seemingly frozen in perpetual motion, are exceptionally powerful images. Moreover, they are not just symbols of the Dao [Tao] but, since they too are part of the web of existence and subject to the inevitable processes of time and decay, actually part of the Dao [Tao] they represent.

Imbued with *Ch'i*, the symbolism of the garden was representational of nature, and as with nature in harmony with the rhythms of the changing seasons. Through developing the garden's harmony the receptive scholar could both develop his own harmony and contribute positively to the harmonious balance of the universe. And in a very Confucian way a garden also had an ethical influence. An example of this is noted by Cooper who quotes the Qianlong Emperor (r. 1735–96) praising gardens because they had, 'a refreshing effect upon the mind and regulated the feelings', thus preventing man from becoming 'engrossed in sensual pleasures and losing strength of will'.

OPPOSITE In the centre of this painting on silk from the Song dynasty (c.983) showing the six paths to rebirth and the ten kings, the Bodhisattva Ksitigarbha is seen sitting on a lotus blossom.

LEFT A rock formation in the Lion Forest Shizilin garden. As well as large *taihu shi* placed in gardens scholar-gardeners also indulged in petromania and displayed collections of smaller, fantastically-shaped rocks on tables in garden courtyards.

# Liú Yuán (The Lingering Garden)
## Suzhou, Jiangsu province, China

In a city that is blessed with a number of beautiful and diverse scholar or classical gardens, *Liú Yuán* (The Lingering Garden) stands out as one of the finest, and, at 2.3 hectares (5½ acres), one of the largest. The garden was first laid out in the sixteenth century, then reconstructed and enlarged in the eighteenth and nineteenth before undergoing a major restoration in the twentieth. It is a delightful (if somewhat disorienting) experience to explore the garden. The layout is deliberately such that the garden continually changes as one moves through the complex of buildings, courtyards and garden pavilions via paths, covered walkways, rockeries and bridges. Not only does the garden open and close but the scale continually varies too — from the expansive lake to tiny courtyards planted with a single banana plant. This is a sophisticated

work of art that also unites the essential religio-symbolic components of the Chinese scholar's garden, for instance the apparent dislocation is deliberate, an earthly expression of the diversity of the infinite cosmos.

Constructed for the court official Xu Taishi in 1593, what is now called the Middle Garden was the first to be made. It is hard to discern that the enclosed space is in fact square because one's eye is drawn to the stylised naturalistic 'rural idyll' of the informal lake backed by the man-made mountain (created by the noted artist Zhou Binzhong), the delightful pavilions and the wisteria-clad bridges. Here the religio-symbolic use of water and rock combine with the plantings of trees, evergreen shrubs, bamboo, banana, peonies and climbers to create and capture the sense of cultivated natural landscape. The garden unites

perfectly with the buildings to bring man and nature in accord to create that indeterminate quality of a scholar's garden — peaceful harmony. Beyond the western wall the garden was extended to include a naturalistic landscape with pavilions, a large artificial hill and a collection of over 500 *penzai* (or Chinese bonsai). To the east is the delightful courtyard called the Small Garden of Stone Forest with its composition of sculptural rocks and evergreen shrubs. However, the most significant feature in this part of the garden is found within a courtyard to the north of the Old Hermit Scholars' House. Here are the Three Peaks, three (very valuable) examples of *taihu shi* monoliths. The Cloud Capped Peak (*Guan Yun Feng*) stands 6.5 metres (21 feet) tall and is the tallest example of a *taihu shi* in all of Suzhou's gardens.

OPPOSITE The moon gate at the end of a long, straight, bamboo-lined path that leads from the courtyard to the north of the Old Hermit Scholars' House which contains three huge *taihu shi* to the Small Garden of Stone Forest.

LEFT Throughout the garden small windows frame vignettes of plants and rocks, and contribute to what to the Western mind is a disorientating experience but which is supposed to represent the cosmos.

# Japan

Very few famous places that are so familiar as images exceed all expectations when experienced in person. The Taj Mahal is one example, the Giza pyramids are a second, and the 'dry garden' within the temple complex of *Ryōan-ji* in Kyōto, is a third. Such a 'Zen garden' is what most Westerners equate with 'Japanese gardens', but to do so is to miss their deeper significance. Moreover such gardens are not the only expression of Japanese garden art with a religio-significance.

The ancient Japanese indigenous and ritualistic belief system is Shinto, meaning 'The Way of the Spirits'. With its deep reverence for nature and nature's beauties it continues to play a central role in Japanese life. Shinto is not a doctrine to explain the universe, in fact it has no canonical scriptures. Nor does it differentiate between a physical and a transcendental; it teaches that everything, including the spiritual, is experienced as part of this world. The vehicle and mechanism by which this holistic natural world both sacred and material (the invisible and visible) is interpreted are the *kami*. *Kami* include gods and spirit beings but are not only gods and spirit beings. Rather they are individual, invisible and positive forces or 'spirits' that reside in all things (as distinct from the Taoist *Ch'i* which is the one force that permeates all things). It is believed that *kami* are a positive force concerned with human welfare. They want us to be happy and if properly revered with rituals and devotion they will intercede benignly.

Basically *kami* are of two types: ancestral spirits and those which pervade specific objects or phenomena (for example, wind, thunder, storms and earthquakes; the sun, mountains, rivers, trees, and rocks). Through the devotion to the latter, Shinto is distinguished by a delight in the beauties of and reverence for nature. Certain unique or extraordinary natural objects and places are considered to have an especially strong sacred spirit and are held as an interface between man and the *kami*. Such objects of ritual worship or *go-shintai* may be an unusually-shaped rock (at Ise in Mie Prefecture), a gnarled

tree weathered over the centuries, a strikingly jagged or perfect mountain (Mount Fuji) or a waterfall of unusual shape or size. A shrine is placed near to or surrounding the venerated object and houses (enshrines) the *kami*. Shrines are thus sacred spaces separate from the ordinary, normal world. *Torii* gates demarcate public routes to the shrine while the boundaries separating the shrine from the ordinary are both symbolic – for example, statues of protection – and real – for example, ropes and the *niwa*. *Niwa* is in fact the Japanese word for garden and its etymology can be traced first to meaning a sanctified space in nature set apart for the worship of Shinto and thence to include the expanse of white gravel on which a Shinto shrine is placed. Thus from the outset the Japanese garden has had a meaningful and close religious association with nature.

OPPOSITE Mount Fuji is not only an iconic image of Japan but it is also one of the most sacred sites within the Shinto belief system.

RIGHT A Japanese woodblock print in Ukiyo-e style shows an historical representation of the Shinto shrine of Meoto-iwa at Futamiura, Ise. The shrine as it is today is shown over the page.

# Ideas arrive from China

Taoism with its immortality and Isles of the Blessed mythology together with Buddhism (and its Hindu influences) are the two imported belief systems that have and continue to have a strong influence on Japanese garden-making; and both came to the land of the rising sun from mainland China. The former had arrived by the late fifth century AD for an entry of 478 in the *Nihon shoki* ('Chronicles of Japan', *c.*720) claims that the Isles of the Blessed were reached by the son of Urashima. Buddhism has been practised in Japan since 552 but may have been introduced earlier duing the Kofun period (*c.*250–538). It established quickly and in 594 was officially recognised during the regency of Prince Shōtoku (regent 593–622).

The introduced blend of Taoist and Buddhist nature reverence was enthusiastically studied and coexisted harmoniously alongside Shinto with its powerful sense of nature. Indeed in many ways they complemented one another. To put this in context, Buddhism arrived in Japan at approximately the same time that Christianity was introduced from mainland Europe into another large offshore island, Britain. Here the dominant pagan religions were nature-centric, polytheistic and not wholly dissimilar to Shinto. In Japan the new ideas coexisted with the old and Buddhist temples were often erected next to Shinto shrines. This would be analogous to finding a Druidic grove and sacrificial altar next to the village church. But the cooperation goes deeper than the mere physical. In medieval Japan *kami* were considered guardians or students of the Buddha's *dharma* or teaching, even manifestations of Buddha. The equivalent would have been the medieval Christian Church accepting that the old gods were guardians or students of the gospel of Christ, or even the spirit of Christ in an indigenous form.

OPPOSITE Stepping stones cross the pool at Naka Shin-en (Middle garden) at the Heian period Jingu Shrine in Kyōto. The reason for their staggered route is the belief that evil spirits could only cross water in a straight line.

BELOW An example of the *yarimizu* or river-style garden is the restored eighth-century *Kyuseki Teien* on the site of the Heijo imperial palace at Nara.

OVERLEAF Always respectful of nature Japanese garden-makers have a rich palette of plants from which to choose. This spectacular display of native maples in full autumnal blaze is at *Daigo-ji*, a Shingon Buddhist temple in Fushimi-ku.

# Nara period (710–94)

Throughout the Nara period Japanese society remained mainly rural, agricultural and village-based. Power was held in the imperial court with the first capital constructed at Nara (710). Administrative and economic activity increased, as did factional infighting at court resulting in the decline of imperial power. Culturally, literature blossomed with the first national histories produced (including the *Nihon shoki*) along with various collections of poetry. Now well established, Buddhism, or rather its monks, gained power at court and gardens were made. And as with the other visual arts and architecture the Japanese practised a cultural appropriation that ran in conjunction with a talent for reinvention. The following focuses on the religious aspect of Japanese gardens but for those wishing to study the garden history of Japan in a broader context Nitschke's excellent volume is much recommended.

No original Nara gardens survive but archaeology has revealed examples of *yarimizu* or river-style gardens (see p.127). These featured a sinuous meandering stream whose course is punctuated by carefully placed rocks simulating the natural obstacles, constrictions and falls found along a mountain stream. The restored eighth-century *Kyuseki Teien* found on the site of the Heijo imperial palace at Nara is edged with fist-sized water-washed cobbles and was overlooked by a pavilion to the west. Such designs drew heavily for their inspiration on Chinese naturalistic prototypes of the Tang dynasty which were dominated by lakes with islands and rock groupings indicative of mountains. Although using religio-motifs and programmes from China these were secular gardens for pleasure. Nevertheless these prototypes were subsequently incorporated into Pure Land gardens, for example the pond garden at *Mōtsū-ji* featured a *yarimizu*.

# Heian period (794–1185)

With the ascent of Emperor Kammu in 781 there followed a period of centralisation of political powers and in 794 a new capital was established at Heian-kyō about twenty-six kilometres (16 miles) north of Nara. Now known as Kyōto, the 'Capital of Peace and Tranquillity' remained there until the 1868 Meiji restoration reinstated imperial rule. Kyōto was sited and aligned (north/south) according to the geomantic principles of *feng shui* imported from China and its hierarchical layout was based on the Tang capital of Changan.

OPPOSITE The beautiful Pine Isles in Matsushima Bay are an example of a location of Shinto reverence that was often miniaturised and recreated within gardens.

BELOW The contemporary photograph shows that little has changed in Amanohashidate, the long peninsula extending into Miyazu Bay, since Utagawa Hiroshige produced his print in the mid-nineteenth century. This, one of the three famous views in Japan was also a popular inspiration for the creation of tree and rock arrangements within gardens.

In the ninth century the Fujiwara clan came to dominate political power. Although sovereignty nominally remained with the emperors (they ascended in their minority and conveniently resigned when reaching their majority), it was the Fujiwara regents who wielded power. Both the members of the somewhat under-employed imperial court and the ruling nobility had the time, wealth and inclination to patronise the arts, which in turn flourished. At the same time contact with China declined and local art and literature, while retaining references to its classical Chinese origins, began to develop its own expression and style.

The *yarimizu* garden became increasingly influenced by local natural landscapes, and garden scenes became more complex. But the garden was not simply a re-creation of nature using artificial means. The Japanese began to perceive and pursue as an expression of beauty the overlapping perfections of a natural object and the man-made type. Nature crafted by man and, at its best, nature as art. A third

form of nature in many ways analogous to that expressed in the Italian Renaissance garden, but which in Japan also evolved as a very *yin-yang* duality between the artistic expression of the natural form in the garden and the architecture's geometric shapes. Symbolism also continued to be expressed within these naturalistic gardens. Be it the miniaturisation and re-creation of a particularly Shinto-revered or auspicious Japanese scene, for example the Pine Isles in Matsushima Bay (in northern Honshu near the city of Sendai) or an arrangement of trees and rocks that evoked literary and philosophical references such as Amanohashidate (in Miyazu Bay in northern Kyoto Prefecture), or *hōrai*, rocky structures that resembled the mythological Islands of the Blessed, Mount Meru, or Mount Fuji herself. It can be said that the emotional and artistic (as supposed to the intellectual and religious) attitude of the Heian nobility towards nature was *mono no aware*. This untranslatable concept embraces a sensitivity towards beings, and thus all objects. Of highest regard, though were mountains. For whether artistically capturing the essence of indigenous natural scenes or replicating elements from Taoist or Buddhist-Hinduist cosmology, all stylistic approaches to the design of Japanese gardens down the centuries have placed a high symbolic value on mountains. To quote Nitschke:

> Touching the soul of the Japanese islanders [profoundly was] the powerful image of the mountain at the centre of the universe and of the waters of both life and death. Mountain and water converge in the image of the island, which appears in Japanese cosmology – as indeed else-where – as the first manifestation of land, indeed of form as such. The recurrent appearance of the cosmic mountain throughout the history of the Japanese garden points to the resonance which the simplicity, power and beauty of this pre-scientific model of the universe finds in the collective Japanese subconscious.... Just as the ancient

civilizations of East Asia built stupas, temples, even entire cities in the shape of the mandala, symbol of the structural principles of the cosmos as a whole, so it comes as no surprise to find this same mandala, with the axis mundi at its centre, inspiring the design of many a Japanese garden.

Reverence for nature expressed as beauty through nature-as-art is one of two broad but parallel schools of thought governing garden design expounded in the *Sakuteiki* ('Records of garden making'). This, the earliest known Japanese text concerned with garden-making, dates to the eleventh century and was purportedly written by Tachibana no Toshitsuna (1028–94), third son of Fujiwara no Yorimichi, who founded the temple of Byōdō-in (see p.138).

RIGHT Just as in China the natural landscape also inspired art forms as well as garden making, so Utagawa Hiroshige's print depicts a traveller on a steep mountain pass on Mount Kaito with blossoming trees and a distant view of the sea.

BELOW Detail from the stone garden or *kare-sansui* in *Nanzen-ji* temple, Kyōto. Note that the gravel is a special type of coarse granite sourced from a nearby river.

The second approach is the Sino-centric one of Taoist mythological metaphors, Buddhist influences and *feng-shui* geomantic principles. Thus according to the translation by Jiro Takei and Marc Keane of chapter eight which deals with 'Garden Streams':

> When one is trying to select a site with correct geomantic conditions, remember that the place on the left side where water runs from is called the Land of the Blue. Similarly, water should run from the east of the Main Hall or outer buildings, then turn south and finally flow out to the west. In the case of water that flows from the north the stream should first be brought around to the east and then caused to flow to the southwest.

> It was believed that 'the waters from the Blue Dragon will wash all manner of evil off to the Great Path of the White Tiger'.

RIGHT In this scene from *The Tale of Genji* the contrast between the natural elements and the linearity of the architecture mirrors the tension between Genji's true desires and his social responsibilities. The lush natural setting of the pavilion typifies aristocratic residences on the outskirts of Kyōto in the early Muromachi period.

BELOW A colour woodcut by Kunisada (1860) shows a richly-robed Prince Genji sat in an elegant pavilion enjoying the vista of an autumnal garden and listening to the cricket's song while a young female attendant pours him sake.

Lakes were dug in the shape of an auspicious word written in the cursive script, for example water (*mizu*) or heart (*hokoro*), while crossings and bridges became important guards against evil spirits. It was believed these could cross water but only in a straight line, hence the popular use of stepping stones and zigzag bridges. Certain naturalistic rocky islands (as well as the lakes in which they stood) or rocky outcrops within the garden itself were constructed to suggest the form of a crane or turtle and thus introduced strong symbolic overtones of the Immortals. *Tsuru-jima* or 'crane islands' (in recognition of the birds upon whose back the Immortals flew) were characterised by mounds, with rocks or pine trees depicting a bird in flight; and *kame-jima* or 'turtle islands' (representing the beasts upon whose backs the Isles were carried) were composed of a rock resembling the head, four less prominent rocks as the flippers and sometimes a sixth for the tail. Both features also came to be symbolic of longevity.

BELOW A rock arrangement creates a turtle island in a lake, complete with fountain. In many cases the subject was more subtly depicted so that its form was not so immediately obvious. One had to 'read the garden'.

Another rare and fascinating literary survivor from the eleventh century offers further insight into this second approach. *The Tale of Genji*, sometimes called the world's first modern novel was written between 1001 and 1020 by Murasaki Shikibu (c.978–c.1014 or 1025) a noblewoman and lady-in-waiting at the imperial court. As well as offering unique insight into court life and culture at the time, the text also describes Prince Genji in various garden settings. For example, he admires the autumn show of leaf colour and boats on island-filled lakes. One passage in particular indicates that the prince not only envisaged his courtly ladies as personifications of the qualities of their favourite gardens but also that he built his palace in the form of a mandala, with each of the four gardens of his four favourite ladies corresponding to the cardinal point appropriate to their season.

Nitschke is tempted to conclude from this description that: 'the rules of geomancy governed not only the design of the capital and the imperial palace but even the gardens of the nobility, and that these, too, were intended to represent a sort of mandala, an image of the universe'.

# Pure Land gardens

The Sino-centric expression of garden influences also resulted in symbolic gardens made in the image of the Isles of the Blessed or the Pure Land of the Amitābha Buddha. The popularity of a doctrine that offered a moderately effortless way to a permanent rebirth in a paradise landscape may also have been influenced by anxiety caused by a *fin-de-siècle* feeling or more accurately *dharma*-ending period in the twelfth century when internecine war and civil strife ravaged the country.

Like their Chinese antecedents the sophisticated nobility and imperial court of the later Heian period generally designed their own aristocratic residences and associated gardens. The buildings followed the dictates of the *shinden-zakuri* style of architecture which itself was a copy of the Pure Land representations of paradise. This had its first expression in the imperial palace erected in the new capital of Kyōto. The main, central building (the *shinden*, literally 'sleeping hall') invariably faced south and was joined to an array of subsidiary buildings by covered corridors and bridges. The overall complex was often linear in organisation, except for the pair of perpendicular corridors that terminated in a *tsuri-dono* or fishing pavilion on one side and an *izumi-dono*

or spring pavilion on the other. The resulting U shape was symbolic of the ideal, embracing, 'armchair' shape desired by geomancy. The buildings were connected to one another and to the garden with an open fluidity that blurred the boundary between indoor and outdoor spaces. It is a style that contrasts strongly with the solid mass of Western architecture and is even more light and airy than its Chinese counterpart. The *chitei* or pond garden was located to the south of the *shinden*. Modelled on a Chinese prototype it had a clearly discernible religious iconography. In the most explicit and structured sense it was a picture of paradise. The *tsuri-dono* and *izumi-dono* embraced the *nantei* or sand-covered foreshore of the lake in front of the *shinden*. With its strong echoes of the *niwa* (the expanse of gravel in front of a Shinto shrine) it served as a stage for performances of theatre, mime and dance. The lake itself, fed by a small stream which entered the garden in the north-east corner according to geomantic principles, featured one or more islands. But no longer did the central island symbolise that of the Taoist Immortals far out in the eastern sea but rather, connected to the southern and northern shores (earth) by arched vermillion bridges that signified the path to

LEFT Pure Land gardens in Japan were more richly planted that those of the subsequent Zen Buddhist-inspired ones.

OPPOSITE AND OVERLEAF *Oizumi ga ike* pond in the garden of *Mōtsū-ji* temple takes advantage of its natural setting.

paradise, it now represented the Pure Land itself. Thus what developed was a highly mandalistic form of garden within which each feature – trees, rocks, mountain shapes, lakes, islands and bridges – was assigned a specific, systematised significance referencing accession to the Pure Land.

Such paradise gardens were also well planted with many more taxa than in subsequent periods. Black pines (*Pinus thunbergii*) and red pines (*P. densiflora*) were popular subjects for island planting, and species such as Japanese maples (*Acer palmatum*), ornamental cherries and herbaceous species were used to introduce seasonal variations to the scenes. *Sakura* or ornamental cherries have for many centuries held a special delight for the Japanese and *o-hanami* or blossom-viewing parties continue to be a national pastime, as do viewing the autumn colours of the Japanese maples. The Japanese also adopted the symbolism of the Chinese 'Three Friends of Winter' (see p.116) but with the exception of lotus grown in ponds with its Buddah-association there was no overt religio-symbolism to the planting of these paradise gardens.

Moreover, the boundary between the religious paradisiacal Pure Land gardens and the secular pleasure gardens of the nobility was fluid. Or perhaps it was in anticipation of the promised delights of the paradisiacal afterlife that the garden was also enjoyed as a pleasure ground, a setting for personal amusement, courtly festivities, banqueting, poetry competitions and boating parties. Indeed, certain Japanese art historians sum up these elegant, colourful and joyful places as *chisen shuyu teien* or 'pond-spring-boating-garden'. That is to say a garden with a spring- or stream-fed pond designed to be viewed and enjoyed (at least in part) from the water. Just such a boating party given in Murasaki's spring garden is delightfully described in chapter twenty-four of the *Tale of Genji*. From this point on they composed poem after poem in an attempt to capture the beauty of the moment.

There are very few extant examples of Heian Pure Land gardens but *Byōdō-in* (Temple of Equality and Impartiality) in Uji, to the south of Kyōto, survives as the oldest example and its wooden Phoenix Hall (1053) as the prime extant example

of the *shinden* style of architecture. Sadly though, while both remarkable and beautiful, the hall and its surrounding landscape retain only a fraction of their former grandeur. The original villa complex built by Fujiwara Michinaga and enlarged by his son Yorimichi comprised twenty-six halls and seven pagodas grouped around a much larger pond. A later survivor that has recently been restored is the twelfth-century pond garden at the temple of *Mōtsū-ji* near Ichinoseki in Iwate Prefecture. Laid out according to the precepts set down in the *Sakuteiki* the pond is called *Oizumi ga Ike* and as well as the Pure Land symbolism there is an artistic nature element as the rocks are arranged to represent the dramatic and beautiful nearby coast: a peninsular beach, rocky coastline, mountains and islands protruding from the lake.

Two significant Kyōto gardens which have a Pure Land origin but have since been modified are *Ginkaku-ji* (Silver Pavilion) where the single pavilion stands at the head of a small naturalistic landscape of streams, islands and lakes, and the much larger and earlier *Kinkaku-ji* (Golden Pavilion).

Here the exquisitely beautiful Mirror Lake with its islands created in the very early fifteenth century is now one of the finest garden expressions of another, more ambitious, Buddhist cosmology – the Indian *cakravala*. This cosmology espouses that the universe is a circular disk that rests on a foundation of golden earth which in turn floats on water. At the centre, the *axis mundi*, is Mount Meru and around it in concentric circles are a series of seven circular golden mountain ranges separated by eight oceans. At the perimeter is the *cakravala* or wall of iron. Only in the ocean between the seventh mountain range and the *cakravala* are there four islands inhabited by man (a further eight uninhabited islands float in the other oceans). This cosmography was adopted into the Japanese garden where Mount Meru is often represented by a single, prominently-located and towering rock, sometimes surrounded by subsidiary stones. In other cases, the representation of all eight mountain ranges and oceans underlies the design of the entire garden, and this is what may be seen at *Kinkaku-ji*.

BELOW The spectacular Phoenix Hall was once at the centre of the Pure Land garden at *Byōdō-in* temple. The garden is reduced but the hall is a unique survivor of eleventh-century *shinden* architecture.

RIGHT Nestling at the back of its intimate and aesthetically delightful Pure Land garden is the Silver Pavilion. Both are now a part of the larger garden complex of *Ginkaku-ji,* Kyōto.

OVERLEAF *Kinkaku-ji* boasts one of Kyōto's most spectacular landscapes. Here the striking (albeit rebuilt) Golden Pavilion is reflected in the waters of the Mirror Lake, which together with its contingent of islands is an expression of the Buddhist *cakravala*.

# Zen

The dominant clan of the Heian period, the Fujiwara, declined in the twelfth century with the Minamoto clan gaining ascendency following their victory in the Genpei War (1180–85). They established their headquarters at the town of Kamakura, which gave its name to their period of dominance. The Kamakura period (1185–1333) marked the beginning of the Japanese medieval era, a nearly 700-year long epoch during which the emperor, the court, and the central government were left intact but largely relegated to ceremonial functions. This was an era when both a new social class and a new religio-philosophical ethic rose to dominance. Each had an enormous impact on religious garden design and evidence

The extensive temple complex of *Daitoku-ji,* Kyōto contains a number of sub-temples that are home to a diverse collection of both historic and contemporary *kare-sansui.* The example in *Daisen-in* (opposite) seems to show a mossy shoreline with promontories and bays together with islands set within a 'rough sea' of raked gravel. In contrast the example at *Ryugen-in* (below) appears a more traditional composition.

of them survives from the subsequent Muromachi period (c.1337–1573). Instead of ruling through a puppet regent the Minamoto established the first shogunate in which political and military power resided with the warlord-head of the samurai government. The origins of the samurai or warrior class date to the Heian period when, in order to protect themselves during the general instability that marred the country from the ninth century on, the provincial upper class owners of *shōen* – privately owned and autonomous (tax free) rural estates or manors – evolved into a new military elite.

Running in parallel with this social change was the rise of a particular Buddhist sect called *Chán* in China and Zen in Japan. Introduced in 1191 by the monk Eisai, the sect's dedication to austerity, simplicity,self-discipline and training appealed to the needs and wants of the samurai. Zen provided them with a philosophical framework and it prospered under their sponsorship. As power decentralised into feudal fiefdoms cultural life shifted away from royal and noblemen's palaces to the villa residences of the samurai, retired Shogun and

Zen monasteries which they sponsored. Concurrent was the architectural evolution from the symmetrical *shinden-zukuri* palace to the asymmetrical and more modest *shoin-zukuri* villa inspired by the architecture of the Zen temple and new domestic requirements that juxtaposed residential needs with areas devoted to display and entertainment. The oldest extant *shoin* style building is the *Tōgu-dō* at *Ginkaku-ji* in Kyōto which dates from 1485. The expression of the garden also evolved as its relationship with both architecture and

user changed. The large Heian paradise garden gave way to smaller gardens integrated within spaces in front of and between the *shoin-zukuri*. Thus the user ceased being a participant and became instead a viewer of a garden not to be entered. Certainly the reductive aesthetic of Zen was a driving force for this change, but so too was the purpose and meaning of the Zen garden, which may be called 'contemplative', although this is not to say that such gardens were not also enjoyed for their artistry.

ABOVE Juxtaposed with the Pure Land garden at *Ginkaku-ji* (see p.139) is an unusual *kare-sansui*. Here, sea and mountain were for the first time both represented in gravel. The *kogetsudai* (above) represents Mount Fuji and the *ginshanada* (below), a raised expanse of coarse silver gravel, the sea.

PARADISE GARDENS

# New paradigm

More commonly called *Kokedera* or the Moss Temple because of the many different types of moss growing there, the garden of the *Saihō-ji* temple in west Kyōto marks a paradigm shift in the religio-garden form. For here, dating to 1339, is an upper garden composed of a series of rock arrangements which some scholars identify as the first Japanese expression of a Zen-inspired garden; certainly it is the oldest extant example of *kare-sansui* ('withered-mountain-water garden'). There is, however, academic debate concerning when this new form first emerged, for in chapter four of *Sakuteiki*, entitled 'Stones', it states that:

> There is also a way to create gardens without ponds or streams. This is called the Dry Garden Style [*kare-sansui*] and should be created by setting stones along the base of a hill or with Meadows in the garden.

Some argue, therefore, that the dry garden is a development of this and not an invention of the Kamakura or Muromachi periods. Be this as it may, *Saihō-ji* marks the emergence of a new prototype, albeit one that retains features of earlier influences. There is a lower pond garden of a reduced size (technically a *chisen kaiyu shiki* or 'pond-stroll garden' as opposed to the *chisen shuyu teien* or 'pond-spring-boating garden'), and the garden as a whole is intended to be entered and explored.

BELOW, RIGHT AND OVERLEAF *Saiho-ji* temple, Kyōto is now most famous for its moss garden, but here in 1339 was made what scholars consider the first Zen-inspired garden.

By the end of the Muromachi period the *kare-sansui* had evolved into a new garden style. An extremely creative, powerful, disciplined and revolutionary form conditioned by artistic and iconographic expression united with a religious intent. Zen teaches that enlightenment through meditation is achieved through *ji-riki* or 'power from oneself'. That is to say the focus of contemplation and the meditative state is introspective. The abstract *kare-sansui* is a vehicle to achieve this as the contemplative viewer is drawn into the composition and begins a metaphysical journey to the self. Certain *kare-sansui* also have a discernible iconography and symbolism. For example juxtaposed to the pond-stroll-garden in *Ginkaku-ji* is a *kare-sansui*. Here for the first time both ocean and mountain are symbolised only with sand — the former by the *ginshanada* (silver-sand-open-sea), a raised expanse of coarse white sand raked to suggest waves, and the latter by the *kogetsudai* (platform facing the moon),

a flattened cone of sand purportedly representing Mount Fuji. Exactly when they were created is not known but it was probably sometime in the century preceding their first reference, a poem dating to 1578. Sometimes the garden may be 'read' on more than one level. For example, the garden at *Daisen-in* (a sub-temple of the extensive *Daitoku-ji* temple complex in Kyōto) that surrounds the north-south aligned *hondo*, or main hall, obeys the north-east to south-west rules of Heian geomancy and displays a series of Taoist and Buddhist-inspired vignettes. Mount Horai (Penglai in Chinese) is depicted by a clipped camellia, its rivers by gravel, a turtle and baby-turtle island, the 'middle sea', and a lonely

bodhi tree. At a deeper level the garden is symbolic of the course of human life. On a third level, there is the distillation of natural landscapes and the aesthetic expression of their essential essence which Nitschke argues is deliberately present, suggesting that whilst the Heian garden:

> imitates the outer forms of nature within a selective landscape of natural features…the Muromachi garden takes a step further: it seeks to imitate the inner forms of nature and thereby fathom the secret laws of its proportions and rhythms, energy and movement. Its means a abstract [*sic*] compositions of naturally-occurring materials.

But there is not always an easy answer when it comes to interpreting *kare-sansui* – and perhaps this is the point. The most famous and most beautiful example is also the most enigmatic. Umpteen theories have been proposed to explain the arrangement of the rocks at *Ryōan-ji* but the most rational and apposite is that (to coin the Modernist maxim) 'form follows function'. The purpose of the garden was (and is) to be a meditative tool, a preternatural vector which, if focused on, induces meditation. In this state it is possible to reverse the outflowing of personal energy to an inward focus on the consciousness. This in turn facilitates introspection and the personal insight of impartial awareness: of the void. Thus the garden's design symbolises neither a natural nor a mythological landscape, rather it symbolises nothing. It is *mutei*, 'the garden of emptiness'. It is the void.

In conclusion, the fear of death runs deeper than all other fears and goes beyond the bounds of mere history and nations. The religio-archetypes of Chinese and Japanese garden design, based on Hindu cosmology, Chinese myth and philosophy and Buddhist faith, share similarities in their expression, and all have one overriding common theme. To quote Nitschke again: 'They are expressions of man's desire to outwit the laws of nature to which he is subject and to escape death. Paradoxically, man seeks to transcend Nature by means of man-made nature.'

LEFT A picturesque scene where art and nature combine in a Japanese version of a third nature.

RIGHT The point of a Zen garden was as an aid to meditation. Here at *Tofuku-ji*, Kyōto the temple architecture frames the view of the garden and provides visual focus.

# *Ryōan-ji* Temple

## Kyōto, Japan

The temple of *Ryōan-ji* was rebuilt in the aftermath of the Onin civil war (1467–77) during which most of wooden-built Kyōto was reduced to ashes. The reconstruction of the *hōjō* or abbot's quarters was completed in 1499 and the current *kare-sansui* garden probably dates to about this time too. Down the centuries the garden's framework has changed somewhat. Today it is enclosed by buildings and clay walls — the beautiful earthy tones and patina patterns that add to the abstract experience are due to the leaching out of linseed oil added to the clay mix. Yet there is

evidence to suggest that the view from the *hōjō* once incorporated a borrowed landscape beyond. The rectangular garden has also varied slightly in size and now measures about 30 metres by 10 metres (33 by 11 yards).

Sometimes called the highest expression of Zen art and perhaps the greatest masterpiece of Japanese culture the 'garden' is only to be viewed not entered (unless to rake the gravel) and continues to be used as an aid to meditation by the monks of the Myoshinji school of the Rinzai sect of Zen Buddhism who live in the temple complex. The garden itself

BELOW Words cannot convey the psychological experience of being alone in this space and feeling a part of this perfect composition, suffice to say that there is a tangible sense of peace and tranquillity. This view shows the length of the *kare-sansui* garden with behind it the earthy tones of the enclosing wall. The *hōjō* is to the right of the photograph and the garden is to be viewed and contemplated seated on a wooden veranda which down the centuries has been worn smooth by the passing of so many feet (shoes are not allowed in or on Buddhist temple buildings).

RIGHT Part of the view from the *hōjō* veranda that takes in the fourteen visible boulders and rocks, all of which are pieces of art in their own right. The collar of moss surrounding each one highlights rather than detracts from the carefully raked gravel.

BELOW Ryōan-ji is not just about its sublime *kare-sansui*; the temple complex also includes the *Oshidori-ike* or 'pond of mandarin ducks' that boasts two islands and a splendid display of Japanese maples.

LEFT The garden space is now enclosed by a rustic clay wall capped with a tile roof which protects the interesting patterns and hues that add to the abstract visual display and contemplative atmosphere. In times gone by rather than a wall there may have been a view out over a borrowed landscape.

ABOVE The view from the covered walkway that leads down the side of the hōjō and to the veranda frames yet another vision of this remarkable garden. To the right is a separate and verdant moss garden studded with towering bamboos.

contains no plants (except for moss at the foot of the rocks), just an expanse of raked coarse, pale grey granite sand within which are set fifteen boulders and rocks of various sizes. These are aesthetically yet precisely and existentially positioned in five groups — one of five, two of three, and two of two — such that only fourteen are ever visible from ground level. At first sight one could identify the symbolism as a series of islands in a sea; and five, three and two are symbolic numbers within Buddhism. So too is fifteen which denotes completeness, and it is alleged that the fifteenth boulder only becomes visible when the viewer has reached enlightenment.

This tranquil garden, at first glance so simple, is far more abstract and obscure than, for example, *Daisen-in* and, even from the author's purely layman's experiences, there is something deeply metaphysical and psychic about it that is not to be found in other *kare-sansui*.

Yet the *kare-sansui* is not the only garden in the temple complex. Perpendicular to it but separate from it is a verdant moss garden shaded by lofty bamboos and further out in the temple complex is the twelfth-century *Oshidori-ike* or 'pond of mandarin ducks' that boasts two islands. On the larger stands a shrine to Benten, the Shinto goddess of good luck.

# Pantheism and polytheism

## Hinduism and pantheism

All across India and since time *in memoriam* a wide range of different plants have been used in connection with traditional religious customs and beliefs. In fact no ceremony was ever complete without some sacred plant and many were imbued with symbolic meanings and powers that continue to hold sway today. For example, the Santhal people of eastern India use a small fern which they call 'dodheri' (*Cheilosoria tenuifolia*) as a cure against witchcraft and as a protective against the evil eye. While a necklace made of the bark of the petari tree (*Mallotus polycarpa*) is believed by the Oriyan tribe of the Sora peoples of eastern India to protect the nursing mother. The reasons for such beliefs are lost in time but plant symbolism is also significant within Hinduism and continues to be so.

In briefest summary, Hinduism emerged between 500−200 BCE and *c.* AD 300 as the result of a fusion of various Indian cultures and traditions in a process known as the 'Hindu synthesis'. This saw shamanic and Buddhist influences meld with the emerging *bhakti* tradition of personal devotion and religious traditions introduced in the preceding Vedic period (*c.*1750−500 BCE) when an influx of early Indo-Aryan speakers arrived over the Hindukush. Hinduism is polytheistic but is not an organised religion for there is no sole founder nor a single prominent scripture. Rather it is a set of beliefs and a way of life centred on sacred texts, for example the *Rig Veda*, the *Upanishadas* and the *Bhagavad Gita*. Central to Hinduism are the belief in reincarnation (the soul experiencing transmigration through a number of births) and that everything (including humans, deities and nature) is part of a universal, supreme being. Hinduism is therefore

pantheistic. With its etymology derived from the ancient Greek *pan* meaning 'all' and *theos* meaning 'god' there can be a variety of definitions including the concept that the universe and god are identical. Another definition is that everything is part of an all-encompassing, immanent god and all forms of reality may then be considered either modes of that being, or identical with it. Taoism, as described in the previous chapter, is therefore comparable with pantheism.

OPPOSITE Compared with Indian Hindu temples those in Bali, for example the Pura Taman Ayun temple, have a distinct architecture and the complex often includes a garden or gardens.

ABOVE In this opaque watercolour that dates to *c.*1660−70 the goddess Siddha Lakshmi, a Nepalese deity, appears seated on a lotus flower and holds a lotus bud in her left hand. The dark figure to her right is the goddess Kali to whom the red hibiscus is sacred.

(excitable) and *tamas* (indifferent). For example, arka (crown flower, *Calotropis gigantea*) and nandyarvattam (crape jasmine, *Tabernaemontana divaricata*) are *sattva* flowers.

Many plants are also planted in veneration of specific deities. Those with a trifoliate arrangement of leaves such as the varuna (three-leaved caper, *Crateva nurvala*) are symbolic of the *Trimurti*. This is the trinity in which the cosmic functions of creation, preservation and destruction are personified by the forms of Brahma (the creator), Vishnu (the preserver) and Shiva (the destroyer). As in Buddhism both the ashvattha (peepal, *Ficus religiosa*) and lotus have a symbolism in Hindusim. The former is also an example of how a whole host of deities and myths become tied up with a single plant. In this case — and the following is not a complete catalogue — the tree is believed to represent the *Trimurti* — the roots being Brahma, the trunk Vishnu and the leaves Shiva. But also when the demons defeated the gods, Vishnu hid among its branches and thus the tree became his personal symbol too. Another legend has it that Krishna died under an ashvattha tree after which began the present *kali yuga* (this is the last of the four stages the world goes through as part of the cycle of *yugas* described in the Indian scriptures). Would-be mothers make

LEFT In an act of *puja* a marigold garland has been placed over the head of this statue of the elephant-headed god Ganesha.

BELOW From Bilvamangalastava's *Balagopalastuti*, this fifteenth-century colour miniature shows a young Krishna, one of the most widely revered and most popular of all Indian divinities, hiding in a tree and sucking his toes while he contemplates about the world.

Another cornerstone of this nature-loving faith is sacred ceremony, the performance of which requires elaborate ritual in which plants play a central role. For example, *puja* is the act of making a spiritual connection with a deity through invocations, prayers and song to an icon, image or other symbol believed to be imbued with that deity's cosmic energy. An important component of *puja* is the making of an offering in order to seek the deity's blessing. Such offerings are frequently in the form of flowers, petals or a garland of a plant associated with the deity. Red flowers and dūrvā grass (*Cynodon dactylon*) are, for instance, offered to the elephant-headed god Ganesha (rings made of the grass are often worn before starting the ritual of *homa* or sacred fire ceremony), while marigolds (*Tagetes* spp.) are a popular votive to Lord Vishnu who is believed to enjoy the colour yellow. According to Samkhya philosophy such flowers are classified according to one of the three *gunas* or qualities into *sattva* (pure), *rajas*

offerings directly to the tree (a red thread or cloth is tied around the trunk or branches) in order that they may be blessed with a son. And Lakshmi, wife of Vishnu, goddess of wealth, love, prosperity (both material and spiritual) and one of the incarnations of Devi, the mother goddess, is also believed to inhabit the tree, especially on a Saturday! As the epitome of feminine beauty she was supposed to have been born radiant and fully-grown from the churning of the sea (echoes of Aphrodite/Venus) and is portrayed as sitting on her traditional symbol and popular *puja* offering, a lotus bloom. The *Trimurti* are often represented standing on the same flower, but of different colours: white (Brahma), pink (Vishnu) and red (Shiva).

However not all flowers have a positive symbolism. Those of the gudahul (*Hibiscus rosa-sinensis*), for example, are both the favourite flowers for offering to the goddess Kali, the fearful and ferocious form of the mother goddess, and used during incantations of evil designs. These are but a few of the hundreds of auspicious plants offered to or grown for the extensive Hindu pantheon, or whose wood is burned as part of *homa* (for example the aak or crown flower, *Calotropis gigantea*). The full list is too long to explore here; for a detailed catalogue Shakti M Gupta's *Plant Myths and Traditions in India* is recommended.

ABOVE (*from left to right*)
Three of many plants symbolic to Hindus: nandyarvattam (crape jasmine), arka (crown flower) and varuna (three-leaved caper)

LEFT Bowls containing flowers and a small clay dish of food laid as offerings for *puja*.

# Temple gardens

In India Hindu temples often feature a spire not unlike that on a Christian church. It is representational of Mount Meru, the mythical, sacred mountain believed to be the abode of Brahma and the demigods and (as in Buddhism) located at the centre of all the physical and metaphysical universes. Hindu temples are places of pilgrimage rather than congregational worship and Stella Kramrisch observed in *The Hindu Temple* that: 'The gods always play where groves are near rivers, mountains and springs, and in towns with pleasure gardens'.

Thus in rural locations temples are sited near areas of sanctified natural climax vegetation (the culmination stage of plant succession for a given environment) that belong to the tradition of sacred outdoor space. And – as in ancient Greece and pagan Europe – specific Hindu deities (or their avatars) are associated with particular groves, or plants or trees found in them. Sacred groves, sometimes ornamented with statues of their associated deities exist all over India and, taking Tamil Nadu as a specific example, those that are near villages are often dedicated to that village's local gods, the gods of the forest, the snake god, and/or an incarnation of Vishnu. This form of sanctifying nature predates Hinduism and sacred groves continue to have an additional significance as sites of cult activity on occasions such as making offerings to propitiate the *vanadevatas* or forest/tree spirits, to ward off the evil eye and to ask for personal well-being. Today, as well as these continued religious roles, sacred groves also have an important ecological significance and contribute to the preservation of an increasingly threatened biodiversity.

In urban areas, and again taking Tamil Nadu as an example, inscriptions from the Pallava, Pandya and Chola kings reveal that rulers granted areas of land to be dedicated as temple gardens (*thirunandavana* or *nandavanam*) as early as AD 600. Gardeners and watchmen paid for by a special tax were employed to tend and protect such gardens and it was a grave offence in law to interfere with their irrigation systems. The gardens grew a wide range of symbolic plants from which female servants appointed by the king produced the requisite garlands for offerings. Indian Hinduism does not have a tradition of designed ornamental temple gardens but a contemporary exception is the garden complex made at the Akshardham Temple in New Delhi.

## Hinduism in Bali

Hindusim arrived in Indonesia in the fifth century AD where it underwent a level of syncretism with local animistic beliefs, *pitru paksha* or ancestor worship, and aspects of Buddhism. Balinese Hinduism is thus much concerned with a myriad of *hyangs* (local and ancestral spirits) which are thought to be capable of good or harm. Great emphasis is placed on ritual propitiation of *hyangs* through acts of reverence which, it is believed, should be dramatic and aesthetically satisfying. Such acts are often performed at Balinese Hindu temples called *pura*. Unlike Indian temples with their tall spires and enclosed architecture, Balinese temple complexes with their buildings, decorative gates, courtyards and pagoda-like tiered roofs towers or *pelinggih meru* (which as the name suggest are also symbolic of the holy mountain) are places of open air worship. The complexes are also often ornamented with beautiful garden spaces. Built in 1634 by a king of the Mengwi dynasty Pura Taman Ayun, for instance, is a complex of garden terraces and courtyards surrounded by a moat whose overall design symbolises Mount Meru floating in the sea of eternity (see p.156). Equally lovely are the water gardens at Pura Taman Saraswati which is dedicated to Saraswati, the goddess of learning, literature and art.

## The kalpavriksha and Svarga

Apart from the earthly use of flowers and plants as part of Hindu worship, Hindu scripture also contains a mythological tree and a paradisiacal realm. A common trope in Sanskrit literature from the earliest sources onwards is the *kalpavriksha*, a wish-fulfilling divine tree whose branches bear every kind of flower and fruit with the added advantage that the fruits confer immortality. According to various Puranas (or ancient Hindu texts) the *kalpavriksha* was created together with the *kamadhenu* (the divine cow which provides for all needs) during the *samudra manthan* or churning of the ocean of milk. The *kalpavriksha* was subsequently taken to the paradisiacal realm of Svarga by Indra, the Lord of Svarga and god of war, storms and rainfall. Located on and above Mount Meru, this delightful and verdant celestial realm which knows no sorrow, suffering or fear is not so much an afterlife but more a waiting room. A transitory paradisiacal place where righteous, virtuous souls who have performed good deeds in their lives but are not yet ready to attain *moksha* (release from suffering) dwell before their next reincarnation. Here too is to be found an enormous hall in which are hosted slain warriors and which has a similarity with the Norse Valhalla (see p.169).

# Swaminarayan Akshardham Temple
## New Delhi, India

Having taken five years to build, Swaminarayan Akshardham opened in November 2005 in eastern New Delhi and is now a popular landmark in India's cultural and religious landscape. Seventy per cent of all tourists who come to the city visit the temple complex, which, according to the temple's website, 'epitomises 10,000 years of Indian culture in all its breathtaking grandeur, beauty, wisdom and bliss'.

The central temple was designed and built according to the *Pāñcarātra* (Vaishnava Sanskrit Agamic texts) and the *Vāstu Śāstra*. The latter are concerned with the science of architecture and integrate traditional Hindu beliefs, nature, *yantra* (mystical geometric pattern) and a form of geomancy. Certainly the architecture is as beautiful as it is massive, and the complex, in spite of its size and bustle does have a certain spirituality to it. Surrounding the main monument is a lake, the Narayan Sarovar, which contains holy waters from the 151 rivers and lakes that are believed to have been sanctified by Swaminarayan, a modern sect of Hindusim and a form of Vaishnavism. Around the lake's perimeter are 108 *gaumukh* (meaning the mouth of a cow) from which holy water pours and which symbolised the *Janmangal Namavali* or the 108 names for god.

The forty-hectare landscape also boasts the *Bharat Upavan* or Garden of India, a swathe of verdant lawns, manicured trees and shrubs punctuated by stone paths lined with bronze sculptures of the great and the good of India's culture and history. Nearby, the Yogi Hraday Kamal is a lotus-shaped sunken garden with a delightful raised walkway and large monoliths on which are carved quotes from global luminaries including Shakespeare, Martin Luther King and Swami Vivekananda, the ninetheenth-century Hindu monk who did much to introduce the Indian philosophies of Vedanta and Yoga to the Western world.

Particularly beautiful at night is the *Yagnapurush Kund*, which is a modern combination of step well (it is the world's largest at 100 metres square and boasting 2870 steps), musical fountain and a Vedic *yagna kundi* or place for the making of offerings accompanied by chanting of Vedic mantras. During the day the steps provide a place to rest and at night seating for those watching the illuminated fountain show depicting the circle of life.

Dating to 2005 the Askhardham temple, Delhi is not only a vast structure but is, somewhat unusually for an Indian Hindu temple, complemented by an extensive garden and lake complex. Both the landscaping with its associated statuary and the water have a strong religious significance as well as creating an aesthetically pleasing setting for the temple building.

# European paganism

As already noted, sacred groves played a significant role in the expression of Indian Hindu religious practices as well as those of Mesopotamia, ancient Greece and Rome. They were also an important component of European Celtic and Norse pagan religious practices. For the purposes of this discussion 'the Celts' can be taken to mean an ethnolinguistic group of tribal societies originally from south-eastern Germany which spread throughout most of the Iberian peninsula and northern Europe (including the British Isles but excluding Scandinavia) and which were a major civilisation for almost a millennium from about 500 BCE. Celtic culture produced exquisitely beautiful works of art but had an oral rather than a written tradition and there is no account of the Celts by the Celts. Mostly accounts are written by their enemy, the Romans, and must be taken with a grain of salt.

The relatively poor transport infrastructure of the time resulted in little long distance land travel and limited communication between tribes and communities. Consequently the expression of Celtic religion varied widely across the continent. Yet in spite of the differences Prudence Jones and Nigel Pennick in *A History of Pagan Europe* identify three shared traits of 'pagan religions': the 'sacred feminine', 'polytheism' and 'nature-based'. That is to say pagan religions recognised 'the female divine principle' identified as 'the Goddess' (as opposed to individual goddesses) besides or

in place of the male divine principle as expressed in the Abrahamic God. They recognised a plurality of divine beings, which may or may not be considered aspects of an underlying unity, and had a concept of the divinity of nature which they viewed as a manifestation of the divine. This latter concept identifies the Celts as animists who believed that every part of nature – trees, plants and even rocks and streams – had its own spirit or divinity and that these spirits or divinities could be communicated with. Such beliefs were therefore more akin to Shintoism than pantheism.

Central to the Celtic way of life and especially sacred were trees. At a practical level trees provided timber for the construction of buildings and the manufacture of wagons, domestic utensils, weaponry and suchlike; wood was a fuel that gave heat and light and certain trees also yielded food and medicines. At a more profound level deciduous trees acted as a reminder of the cycle of the seasons and rebirth while evergreen trees symbolised eternity. And in an age when life expectancy was about thirty years trees had a longevity that it was believed provided a connection with both one's ancestors and the spirit world. Indeed, Celtic creation myths recount that trees were the progenitors of mankind and that the most sacred tree of all, the oak (*Quercus robur*), provided a metaphysical doorway to the Otherworld as well as representing simultaneously the Tree of Life and the world tree or *axis mundi*.

LEFT Recovered from a peat bog the ornate, silver Gundestrup cauldron is held in the National Museum of Denmark, Copenhagen. This detail shows the Celtic god Cernunnos who is thought to have been Lord of the animals, a peaceful god of nature and fruitfulness.

OPPOSITE Growing in Fredville Park, Nonington, Kent the oak tree called 'Majesty' is widely considered to be the most impressive specimen in Great Britain. Legend has it that it is on the site of a Celtic sacred grove, and it is itself some 500–600 years old.

In the first century AD the Roman historian Tacitus wrote that the Germanic tribes did not 'confine the gods within walls . . . but that they worshipped outdoors in sacred woods and groves'. As in India such groves were sanctified areas of climax community forest and in Celtic Gaul (France) were called *nemeton*. The name is associated with Nemetona, protective goddess of the sacred grove who is thought also to have had associations with lightning. Nemetona was one of relatively few deities who was widely revered, evidence of her worship has been found as far apart as England and Germany.

Sacred groves themselves were both inviolate – damaging or felling a tree could result in execution (a punishment also meted out by the ancient Romans, the Norse and Hindus in India) – and spiritually associated with the shamanic activities of druids. The etymology of 'druid' may be hypothetically constructed as a proto-Celtic word *dru-wid-s* meaning 'oak-knower' or someone learned in tree magic. Often of noble birth, druids were the priestly class and held a high position in Celtic society but next to nothing is known about their cult practices. A rare exception is the Ritual of Oak and Mistletoe (*Viscum album*) as it was conducted in Gaul in the first century and recorded by the Roman writer, Pliny the Elder:

> The mistletoe, however, is but rarely found upon the robur [oak]; and when found, is gathered with rites replete with religious awe. This is done more particularly on the fifth day of the moon, the day which is the beginning of their months and years, as also of their ages, which, with them, are but thirty years. This day they select because the moon, though not yet in the middle of her course, has already considerable power and influence; and they call her by a name which signifies, in their language, the all-healing. Having made all due preparation for the sacrifice and a banquet beneath the trees, they bring thither two white bulls, the horns of which are bound then for the first time. Clad in a white robe the priest ascends the tree, and cuts the mistletoe with a golden sickle, which is received by others in a white cloak. They then immolate the victims, offering up their prayers that God will render this gift of his propitious to those to whom he has so granted it. It is the belief with them that the mistletoe, taken in drink, will impart fecundity to all animals that are barren, and that it is an antidote for all poisons.

Another indication of the sacro-magical importance of the tree within Irish Celtic society is the Ogham or Celtic tree alphabet whose use reached a peak in the fifth and sixth centuries AD. Each of the twenty letters was named after a particular sacred tree. For example, the letter 'B' or *Beith* (inscribed similarly to a T) means birch (*Betula utilis*). However most of the examples of the script that survive as stone inscriptions are personal names and cannot therefore be considered a written historical record.

LEFT A somewhat stylised illustration showing Druids ritually gathering mistletoe. According to Pliny the most sacred mistletoe was that growing on oak trees and gathered on the fifth day of the moon with much ceremony.

OPPOSITE Glastonbury Tor which has Celtic and Arthurian associations rises like a beacon out of the Somerset levels and over-looks the Isle of Avalon. In another example of the Christianising of Celtic sites a church was erected on the top in Saxon times. The area is also famous for the Glastonbury thorn (*Crataegus monogyna* 'Biflora') which is linked with legends of Joseph of Arimathea and the arrival of Christianity in England.

# Isles of the Blessed....again

One of several Irish Celtic folklore myths associated with the supernatural Otherworld features Tír na nÓg (or 'Land of the Young'). Sometimes referred to as the Fortunate Isles, this pleasurable island paradise was believed to be far to the west of Ireland. Although it was probably based on the ancient Greek afterlife myth of the Isles of the Blessed, Tír na nÓg has closer parallels with those isles associated with the Chinese legend of the Immortals. For here too there was no sickness, no one wanted for food or drink and all inhabitants enjoyed youthful immortality. However, rather than being inhabited by 'superhumans', Tír na nÓg was primarily the realm of deities, ancestors and powerful spirits. Those mortals who did reside there (and not necessarily permanently) were either questing heroes for whom Tír na nÓg was a sought-after journey's end or courageous champions invited by one of the fairy residents. As Irish mythology spread to England Tír na

nÓg may have been the (joint) inspiration for the legendary island of Avalon which appears in Arthurian legend. Another place famous for its beautiful apples, it was described by Geoffrey of Monmouth in 1136:

> The island of apples which men call 'The Fortunate Isle' gets its name from the fact that it produces all things of itself; the fields there have no need of the ploughs of the farmers and all cultivation is lacking except what nature provides. Of its own accord it produces grain and grapes, and apple trees grow in its woods from the close-clipped grass. The ground of its own accord produces everything instead of merely grass, and people live there a hundred years or more. There nine sisters rule by a pleasing set of laws those who come to them from our country.

# Norse pagan traditions

Norse geography and history (the land was never conquered by the Romans) are distinct from those of the Celts although the two share some of the same chronology. Popular history best remembers the Viking Age (AD 793–1066) but settlement in the general area of modern Scandinavia by proto-Germanic tribes began around 1000 BCE. Thence the Norse developed a distinct linguistic, cultural and religious tradition, but it was an oral tradition like that of the Celts. Most of the earliest written sources describing Norse religio-mythology date to the (post-Christianised) thirteenth century. Valhalla, the Norse version of Elysium was located in Asgard, the realm of the gods. But given the differences in climate between the Mediterranean and Scandinavia it is not surprising that rather than enjoying rolling fields under a balmy sky the glorious dead Norse warrior eternally caroused snug and warm within a great hall. Before Valhalla stood *glasir*, a tree or grove bearing leaves of red gold and described as 'the most beautiful among gods and men'. Indeed, plants played as significant a role in Norse cosmology and mythology as they did in those of the Celts. Ask and Embla, the first man and woman made by the gods, were formed respectively from the wood of the ash (*Fraxinus excelsior*) and elm (*Ulmus glabra*). An alternative etymological derivation of Embla is the vine (*Vitis vinifera*), although the plant is not native this far north and is unlikely to have been in cultivation here during the first millennium BCE. Once again the immortality-giving apple (specifically the crab apple, *Malus sylvestris*) makes an appearance. Eaten by the gods to keep them eternally young the fruit was guarded by Idun or Ithunn, the goddess of spring (aka Chloris). And it was from mistletoe that Loki made the spear (or arrow) that killed Baldr, the god of light and purity.

Baldr was the son of the supreme pair, the god Odin and goddess Frijjō (Frigg) to whom the wood geranium (*Geranium sylvaticum*) and wild strawberry (*Fragaria vesca*) were respectively sacred. And just as the Celts had their tree of life so the Norse had *Yggdrasil*, but rather than an oak it was an eternally

OPPOSITE Lough Gur in County Limerick, Eire is a magical and mysterious place. Its archaeology dates to the Stone Age and some scholars consider it to be the inspiration for Tír na nÓg.

ABOVE RIGHT An eighteenth-century Icelandic illustration derived from the thirteenth-century *Prose Edda* which was compiled in Iceland by Snorri Sturluson. The goat Heiðrún stands atop Valhalla munching leaves of Læraðr, a tree whose meaning is unclear. It may relate to *Yggdrasil* while another translation would suggest it is a 'giver of protection'.

RIGHT In Norse mythology Embla, the first woman, was fashioned by the gods from the wood of the elm tree.

green ash whose branches embraced the nine worlds and extended up and above the heavens, where, at the very top lived an unnamed eagle. *Yggdrasil* was supported by three enormous roots. The first was in Asgard and by this root was Urd's well where the gods held their daily meetings. The second went down to Jotunheim, the land of the giants and by this root was Mimir's well. The third root, upon which the dragon Nidhug endlessly gnawed descended to Niflheim, close to Hvergelmir's well. The eagle and the dragon were bitter enemies and a squirrel named Ratatösk spent much of its time running up and down the trunk delivering messages from one to the other and thus perpetuating their mutual hatred.

The Norse sanctified natural forest spaces but also planted sacred groves around hallowed sites. The German chronicler Adam of Bremen, writing of the Temple of Uppsala in Sweden between 1073 and 1076 and shortly before its destruction, described the sacrificial practices conducted within the grove:

> Of all the living beings that are male, nine heads are offered; by whose blood it is the custom to appease the gods. Their bodies, however, are hung in a grove which is beside the temple. The grove is so sacred to the heathen that the individual trees in it are believed to be holy because of the death or putrefaction of the sacrificial victims. There, even dogs and horses dangle beside people, their bodies hanging jumbled together.

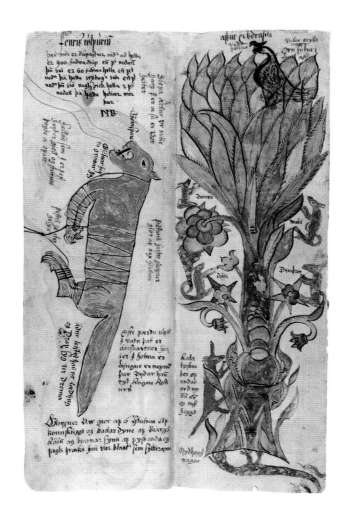

ABOVE RIGHT Nidhug gnaws at the roots of Yggdrasil in an Icelandic manuscript of 1680.

ABOVE The wood cranesbill is sacred to Odin, whose wife was Frijjō (Frigg). She was associated with foreknowledge and wisdom and also gave her name to Friday.

RIGHT A contemporary view looking across the site of Old Uppsala in Sweden. Sadly, neither the temple nor its grove has survived.

# Evergreens

The use of evergreens as a symbol of eternity and rebirth was widespread in early religions. To honour Saturnus, the god of agriculture during the festivities of Saturnalia (December 17) Romans decorated their homes with holly (*Ilex aquifolium*) and mistletoe, which is also thought to be the 'golden bough' of Virgil's *Aeneid*. Ivy, as already noted, was associated with Bacchus. The Norse also paid homage to the holly and the ivy during celebrations associated with the winter solstice recognising them as a symbol of the forthcoming spring while the Celts placed evergreen branches over doors to keep away evil spirits. As Christianity spread across Europe so the early Church assimilated certain pagan traditions, ceremonies, plant symbolism and motifs. Carvings of the enigmatic green man who would appear to be a pagan fertility figure or a nature spirit (with possible Roman origins) was a popular decoration in churches across Europe. The earliest example of a head disgorging vegetation from his mouth dates to about 400 and adorns the tomb of Saint Abre which is now to be found in the church of St Hilaire-le-Grand in Poitiers, France.

During the eleventh century it was popular to enact a Paradise Play on Christmas Eve. It told the Christian creation myth and an evergreen tree hung with apples was an essential prop. When mistletoe was banned as a decoration by the Church in medieval times it was replaced by holly – the prickly leaves representing Christ's crown of thorns and the red berries, his blood. And since at least the fifteenth century when they are both mentioned regularly in churchwardens' accounts, holly has been joined by ivy as a popular Christmas decoration in both church and home. Even that most reformist of monarchs, King Henry VIII wrote a love song 'Green groweth the holly' which uses the evergreen nature of the holly and ivy as an allegory for undying love: 'So I am and ever hath been Unto my lady true'. The familiar and delightful Christmas carol celebrating the pair was first published in a broadsheet in 1710 but is likely to be much older. It may have originated somewhere in the Cotswolds for the melody was collected and saved by the folklore revivalist Cecil Sharp who heard it sung by a Mrs Mary Clayton of Chipping Campden in 1909.

ABOVE LEFT A well-preserved Roman mosaic from Hadrian's Villa in Tivoli, Italy depicts a mask of a somewhat debauched-looking Saturnus crowned with a wreath of ivy leaves and berries.

ABOVE RIGHT A stone carving of a green man with foliage coming from his mouth on a capital in the fourteenth-century church of St Mary's in Finedon, Northamptonshire.

BELOW A stained glass window in the church of St Mary the Virgin, Lapworth depicts holly and ivy. Both plants were given a symbolism by the Church in the fifteenth century.

Since the mid-nineteenth century the coniferous Christmas tree has been the ubiquitous symbol of Yuletide (itself originally a pagan Germanic mid-winter religious festival part of which involved burning a yule log). One legend explaining the origin of this tradition involves the English Saint Boniface (c.675–754) who travelled through Germany as a missionary in the eighth century. One winter's day Boniface came across a group of pagan worshippers gathered around a great oak and about to sacrifice a child. In order to save the child's life Boniface felled the tree which miraculously contained a small fir tree growing inside its rotten trunk. This, the saint told the crowd was a symbol of the eternal life of Christ. However, it is Martin Luther who is generally credited with inventing the Christmas tree decorated with candles, a practice which is continued today in certain northern European countries including Denmark. The story has it that one Christmas Eve in about 1500 Luther was walking through an evergreen forest when he was struck by the beauty of the snow-laden branches glittering in the reflected moonlight. When he got home he decorated a little fir tree with candles in an attempt to recapture the twinkling star-like appearance. But the Christmas tree laden with ornaments and lights as we know it today was a British development of the 1840s led by Queen Victoria whose husband Albert had brought the Christmas tree concept from his native Germany. Many emulated the queen and the popularity of the heavily decorated Christmas tree was further enhanced through the writings of Charles Dickens.

ABOVE A sculptural specimen of the piñon pine grows out of a sheer rock face in Zion National Park, Utah.

BELOW With a buffalo skull at his feet the squatting Slow Bull holds a pipe with mouthpiece pointing skyward and offers a prayer to the Great Spirit.

# North America

The Neolithic or Agricultural Revolution which marked mankind's transition from a nomadic hunter-gatherer existence to a village and agrarian one began in the Fertile Crescent sometime in the eighth millennium BCE. Farming reached southern Europe by the fourth millennium and took another thousand years or so to reach the north. Subsequently it was the Celts who were responsible for spreading the use of iron technology (the Iron Age) across much of the continent. At the same time but on another continent the tribes who inhabited what is now North America continued to pursue a hunter-gatherer lifestyle. Some tribes did develop agriculture but for most, particularly those out on the Great Plains, their nomadic lifestyle changed very little until it was all but destroyed by the arrival and actions of Europeans from the sixteenth century onwards. Nevertheless the traditional spiritual beliefs and ceremonial rituals and practices of the Native Americans which were and are passed down orally

(although many have now also been committed to paper) endured and continue to be practised.

Down the millennia — and in large part due to their relative isolation — individual tribes developed their own histories and sets of beliefs which differ widely across the land mass of North America. Despite their diversity many are distinguished by the importance placed on personal spirituality, a spirituality which is characterised by a strong kinship with and great respect for all aspects of the natural world. Particularly deeply held is the conviction in the interconnectivity between an individual's actions and their simultaneous impact on both the physical natural world and the transcendental spiritual one. These interconnected worlds are, in many ways, characterised by a belief in a supreme being and unifying force that flows in and through all things. This is the Great Spirit or Great Mystery that is known by a range of different names, for example 'Wakan Tanka' to the Sioux, 'Old Man' to the Blackfoot and 'Ababinili' to the Chickasaw. Native Americans believe that all components of the natural world are kindred and brought together by the same Great Mystery (another example of pantheism) and nature is indeed their temple. In contrast to constructed centres of worship or symbolic forms, be they shrines set within planted groves or mandalic rock arrangements in

a garden, this expansive, natural temple is a place where symbolic forms are identified and where each form has a host of precise values and meanings that taken all together constitute what one could call a Native American 'doctrine'.

Plants were of course central to a hunter-gatherer existence but also to rituals and rites. The peace pipe is a clichéd image of Native American ceremony but the ritual of smoking tobacco (*Nicotiana* spp.) and sharing the pipe is very important. Not only is it a practice used to remember and orally transmit tribal history and traditions but it is also believed to be a means of communicating with the spirit. As smoke from the ignited tobacco rises so it becomes the medium for transmitting prayers and invocations from the earth to the astral plane. Many tribes also conducted rituals surrounding the planting and harvest of the tobacco crop.

Another plant used variously by the Navajo is a species of pine know as piñon (*Pinus edulis*). To prepare for the War Dance warriors paint their bodies with pitch from the piñon and willow, while its dried gum is burned as a form of incense during the Mystery of the Night Chant as an act of purification. Desert sage (*Artemisia tridentata*) is also widely used in purification rites, being burned to drive out bad spirits or wrapped around objects — the wrists, ankles and heads of those participating in the Sun Dancer, for instance.

PREVIOUS PAGE Given such beauty as this mountain scene of autumnal foliage and snow-dusted conifers all reflected in the mirror-like waters at Maroon Bells, Aspen, Colorado it is completely understandable how and why Native Americans had and have such a nature-centric belief system.

LEFT A Sioux peace pipe ceremony photographed in the early twentieth century shows the smoking and sharing of tobacco.

OPPOSITE Called *Mató tipila* ('Bear Lodge') in Lakota this striking rocky outcrop is also known as Devils Tower. Located in north-eastern Wyoming and the first declared National Monument (1906) it is a sacred Native American site with associations to over twenty tribes including the Kiowa, Arapaho, Crow, Cheyenne and Sioux.

# Mesoamerica

Mesoamerica is an historico-cultural cohesive area within which a number of pre-Columbian societies flourished until Spanish conquest and colonisation. Geographically it extended approximately from central Mexico to Belize, Guatemala, El Salvador, Honduras, Nicaragua and northern Costa Rica. Chronologically it is divided into five periods: Palaeo-Indian (first human habitation until 3500 BCE), Archaic (3500–2000 BCE), Preclassic or Formative (2000 BCE–AD 200), Classic (200–1000), and Postclassic (1000–1697). The latter date marks the conquest of Tayasal, the last independent native state of Mesoamerica.

It is from the archaeological record that we know what little we do about the oldest of the Mesoamerican civilisations. Often referred to as the founder or mother culture, the Olmec flourished along the southern Gulf Coast of what is today Mexico from about 1200–400 BCE. The Mayan civilisation, which peaked during the Classic period and extended over present-day southern Mexico and parts of the Yucatán Peninsula states as well as Guatemala, Belize, western Honduras and the extreme north of El Salvador, is noted for having the only known fully-developed written language of the pre-Columbian Americas. The Aztec were a collection of ethnic groups in central Mexico (particularly those which spoke the Nahuatl language) which dominated large parts of Mesoamerica between the fourteenth and sixteenth centuries AD. Although restricted to Stone Age technology the Olmec, Maya and Aztec civilisations were significantly more advanced than their Old World counterparts at a comparable stage of their technological evolution and development. For when the *conquistadores* landed in 1519 they encountered sophisticated and massive architecture, beautiful and intricate artworks (sculpture, painting, jewellery, pottery), a complex astronomical and calendrical system, the mathematical concept of zero and an elaborate cosmology. Various comparative techniques – typological analysis of Olmec, Mayan and Aztec iconography and art

OPPOSITE At its zenith in c.250 AD Teotihuacán, Mexico was the largest city in the pre-Columbian Americas. The Avenue of the Dead gives access to the Pyramid of the Moon dedicated to the Great Goddess of Teotihuacan, goddess of water, fertility, the earth, and creation.

RIGHT A scene of human sacrifice from the Codex Magliabechiano. The offering of the victim's heart to the gods satisfied the Aztec belief that the sun would rise again nourished by the hearts of men. Ritualistic 'flowery wars' or *xochiyaoyotl* were conducted not to take land or kill the enemy but simply to capture prisoners for sacrifice.

BELOW A specimen of the giant cotton tree or ceiba which has an unusual, spiny bark and which the Maya considered to be the world tree.

taken with other archaeological finds and written accounts from the Maya and *conquistadores* – have demonstrated that the religions of the three cultures shared certain characteristics. This indicates not only relatively high levels of interaction, cultural diffusion and syncretism, but also the existence of a much older and now lost foundational system of belief.

Mesoamerican religions were sophisticated, complex and polytheistic. The highly diversified and specialised pantheons of hundreds of gods and goddesses were responsible for almost all natural phenomenona, human activities and social groupings. The cosmology centred on the origins and nature of the gods, the creation of man and the universe, the regulation of man's relationship to the gods, and the afterlife. A notable characteristic is a strong dualism (somewhat akin to the Oriental concept of *yin-yang*), with the deities representing confrontation between opposite poles. The positive is exemplified by light, masculinity, movement, war, the sun and so on while the negative is exemplified by darkness, femininity, repose, peace and the moon. Taking care of these deities was an equally large and well-organised priesthood at the head of which was the king. And, as every schoolchild learns, the extensive annual calendar of festival and ritual involved copious bloodshed with an emphasis on human sacrifice and, probably, ritual cannibalism.

As with so many other cosmologies, here too was a world tree which acted as an *axis mundi*. Located in the 'navel of the earth' it penetrated and united three superimposed levels of the world: the upperworld sky realm which was home to most of the gods, the physical earthly realm inhabited by humans, and the underworld, where resided most of the dead. In Mayan religion this cosmic tree was identified as the *yaxche* (ceiba or giant silk cotton tree, *Ceiba pentandra*) and this 'first tree' played a part as a primordial source of human life in Mayan creation myths much as it did in Celtic beliefs. Moreover the Lacandon Maya of Chiapas also believed that each evening the sun descended the roots of the tree to the underworld, while the Tzotzil Maya viewed the sky as a mountain with thirteen steps surrounding a gigantic central ceiba tree.

With the cosmic tree at its centre the earthly realm was united geographically by the four cardinal points thus forming a quincunx pattern. Aztec legend held that at the four corners four additional trees helped support the sky, while on earth certain geographical features and trees came to be considered sacred. Examples might be boundaries such as rivers and the sea, as well as mountains, which were believed to connect the earth to the sky, and caves which were a conduit between the earth and the netherworld. There are parallels here with North American tribal traditions, but in that case the link between the sky and the earth was humans themselves and there was no underworld. Moreover rather than a quincunx the circle, as revealed by such forms as the medicine wheel, was the sacred unifying shape.

Mesoamerican civilisations were agricultural and what wheat was to early farming communities in the Old World so maize (*Zea mays*) was to this part of the New World. And not surprisingly it was similarly revered. One of the Olmec deities has been identified as a maize god and in the better

LEFT An Aztec cosmological drawing from the Codex Fejérváry-Mayer, a rare pre-Hispanic manuscript. In the centre is Xiuhtecuhtli, god of fire and the calendar. At each of the cardinal points around him are other notable deities standing beside a sacred tree.

OPPOSITE ABOVE A sculpture made of clay with a layer of stucco depicting the corn goddess Chicomecoatl holding ripe maize cobs. It is part of a brazier of 1500 to 1520 found fifteen years ago in Tihuac.

OPPOSITE RIGHT The famous statue of Xochipilli, the 'flower prince', seated and seemingly in the grip of an entheogenic ecstasy.

opening communication between the earthly and divine realms, and many hallucinogenic plants and fungi were themselves considered gods. In this case both the base (possibly a drum) and the statue seated upon it are covered in carvings of sacred and psychoactive flora including one of the *teonanácatli* or sacred fungi (*Psilocybe aztecorum*), tobacco, ololiúqui (*Turbina corymbosa*), sinicuichi (*Heimia salicifolia*), possibly cacahuaxochitl (*Quararibea funebris*) and another unidentified flower. The figure himself sits cross-legged, head tilted up, eyes open, jaw tensed, with his mouth half open and his arms opened to the heavens as if in an entheogenic ecstasy.

Xochipilli's twin sister was Xochiquetzal, the Aphrodite-like goddess associated with concepts of fertility, beauty and female sexual power. Unlike several other female earth

understood Mayan cosmology the maize god was perceived as one of the most powerful deities with a rich personal mythology. Indeed, he was originally a she (rather like Demeter) but by the late Classic period (AD 600–900) the goddess had transmogrified in two incarnations: the foliated maize god and the tonsured maize god. The former is thought to represent growing maize and the latter the ripened cobs. According to the sixteenth-century *Popol Vuh* (literally 'Book of the People') – an invaluable source of Mayan mythology which contains both a creation and a flood myth – the hero twins of the epic, Hunahpú and Xbalanqué, have maize plants for alter egos and in an alternative creation myth claimed that man himself was formed from maize. The tonsured maize god also doubled as the tonsured cacao god – a god of chocolate! – and academics have argued that he played a role in the raising of the world tree and thus is central to creation itself. The importance of maize is further revealed by certain Aztec words, deities and rituals. In the Nahuatl language *theocintli* (maize) means 'food of the gods', Chicomecoatl, the goddess of agriculture was the female aspect of Centeotl, the male god of maize, and numerous rituals and festivals were observed around the planting, cultivation, harvest and consumption of maize.

Xochipilli was the Aztec god of flowers (his name literally means 'flower prince') as well as art, games, beauty, dance and song, and is an example of one of many deities with whom non-food plants were directly associated. One statue of Xochipilli is of particular interest. Found on the slopes of the volcano Popocatepetl and dating to the Postclassic period, it suggests that Xochipilli was also the god of entheogenic plants. It is known that psycho-tropic plants were widely consumed as part of many shamanic rituals as a means of

goddesses connected with agricultural and sexual fecundity, Xochiquetzal is always depicted as young, alluring and richly attired. She was also symbolically linked with vegetation and two flowers in particular: izqiuxochitl (*Bourreria huanita*), which was much valued for its fragrant white blooms, its curative properties and as an ingredient of *chocolatl*, and marigolds. Marigold flowers often appear on art works adorning headdresses and were strung into garlands placed over statues of deities.

As was Centeotl the maize god, so too Xochiquetzal was born in Tamoanchan. This verdant, mist-shrouded landscape filled with fountains, rivers and forests was a place of pleasure and, rather like Mesopotamian Dilmun, a paradise garden that was home to the gods who amused themselves with music and dancing. However the blissful tranquillity was interrupted by various creation events that have certain parallels with the Edenic creation myth. For it was here that the feathered serpent god Quetzalcoatl created the first humans from bones which had been stolen from the underworld of Mictlan. Similarly there was a myth of expulsion, not of humans but of younger gods who had disobeyed the supreme

pair's command forbidding them to pick flowers from the tree. Banished from Tamoanchan the errant gods were sent to settle the earth and the world of the dead and give origin to creatures and cycles of life and death. The tree that the guilty gods had violated was symbolically (and confusingly) at one and the same time in Tamoanchan and the world tree itself. For just like *Yggdrasil* in Norse mythology so the Mesoamerican world tree was all embracing and created a cosmic order of which Tamoanchan was an integral part.

At one point in her mythology Xochiquetzal was married to the Tlaloc. With fertility and thunderstorm associations that have a resonance with the Celtic goddess Nemetona, and power over both the munificent and destructive forces of rain and water in general, Tlaloc was a god of particular significance whom the Aztecs worked hard to placate. One of several

OPPOSITE The shrine to Tlaloc the powerful rain god, on Mount Tlaloc, Mexico, with the volcanoes of the Sierra Nevada behind.

BELOW Marigolds were a symbolic plant within Aztec religion and continue to be used in Mexico in various religious festivals such in the creation of artworks to celebrate the Day of the Dead.

festivities dedicated to him was the Festival of Atlcahualo held towards the end of the rainy season and over the (southern hemisphere) autumn equinox. Lasting for a *veintena* (the Spanish-derived name for a twenty-day Mesoamerican month) the festival celebrated renewal through ritual, feast and sacrifice. Michael Graulich identifies the following description of what the sixteenth-century chronicler Fray Diego Durán called 'the Feast of the Tree' in his *Historia de las Indias de Nueva España e Islas de Tierra Firme escrita en el siglo XVI* (1867) as in fact the Festival of Atlcahualo:

> Some days before the feast, people went to the hill of Colhuacan to cut the tallest, fullest and most beautiful tree they could find. They carried it to Mexico with great care, so that no branch would touch the ground, and planted it before the pyramid of Huitzilopochtli and Tlaloc [the Templo Mayor in Tenochtitlan, now Mexico City]. Four lesser trees, forming a square, were placed around the first one which was called Tota, 'Our Father'.

They were tied to each other with ropes and the square was arranged as a artificial garden.

On the eve of the feast, the kings of Mexico-Tenochtitlan, Texcoco and Tlacopan and the hostile rulers of Tlaxcala and Huexotzinco went with a great retinue to the base of the Tlalocan mountain. At dawn they conducted a little boy in an enclosed litter to a shrine of the Tlalocs on top of the mountain. [The most important site of worship was on the peak of Mount Tlaloc, a 4100-metre-high mountain on the eastern rim of the Valley of Mexico] Priests cut the throat of the child, in the litter, 'to the sound of many trumpets, conch shells, and flutes'. The kings and their retinues went in turn to adorn the statues and bring them offerings of quetzal feathers, jade and food, and to anoint them with the victim's blood. Then everybody but a hundred soldiers left to guard the offerings, returned to Mexico.

Meanwhile, in the city a little girl dressed in blue, impersonating Chalchiuhtlicue, goddess of waters, springs, lakes and rivers, had been brought, also in a covered litter, to the artificial garden. There she was set down near the big tree. They sang before her until news arrived that the lords were ready to cross the lake. Then living goddess and the Father tree were conducted to the lakeshore and embarked. At Pantitlan the flotillas coming from the city and the Tlalocan joined each other. The tree was 'thrust into the mud next to the spring or drain' and they killed the little girl by cutting her throat with a pronged harpoon. Her blood nourished the waters and so did her body, which was cast into the whirlpool together with great quantities of jewels, gold, precious stones, feathers and other riches. Then everyone returned home in great silence. The tree was left there until it rotted.

Details from a partly reconstructed wall painting at Tepantitla. The scenes have been interpreted to represent the floriferous paradise of the rain god Tlaloc, where the souls of those especially associated with the god enjoyed a blissful afterlife.

Several Aztec codices (for example the Vaticanus A and Florentine) identify Tlaloc as ruler of Tlalocan, the Aztec paradisiacal afterlife and fourth layer of the heavens (other sources identify Tlalocan as terrestrial and located inside a mountain). Here a parallel can be drawn with the Hindu god Indra, the Lord of Svarga and the paradisiacal realm of Svarga itself.

Tlalocan is described as a place of unending springtime, perpetually green and beautiful, a paradise of flowers and edible plants, this afterlife was available only to those who had died violently as a result of phenomena associated with the god, for example by drowning, water-borne diseases or lightning. Also admitted were victims of child sacrifices and somewhat bizarrely those who had succumbed to leprosy and venereal disease. Interestingly, the Tlalocan-bound dead were not cremated as was the Aztec custom, but instead inhumed with their foreheads painted blue, a digging stick placed in their hands and *huautli* or amaranth (*Amaranthus hypochondriacus*) seed placed on their faces.

*Huautli* was the grain second only in importance to maize and had significant meaning as a fertility symbol and a vehicle of communion with the gods. As well as in the mortuary rite described above the red flowers were used for colouring ceremonial foodstuffs and other religious paraphernalia and may have been a symbol for blood and death. The grains were the main ingredient of tamales (a dish made of a starchy dough steamed or boiled in a leaf wrapper) prepared as ceremonial offerings, and during the winter *veintena* of Atemoztli (also dedicated to Tlaloc) votive statues with bean eyes and pumpkin seed teeth were made out of *huautli* dough. They were adorned, offered fine scents and food, had copal (a native form of tree gum incense) burned before them and were prayed to. Then they were symbolically sacrificed, their doughy chests cut open and their 'hearts' extracted before the bodies were dismembered and ceremonially consumed.

# Gardens of the Gods

This chapter has examined a number of belief systems in which nature was or is considered sacred, which imbue(d) plants with a strong symbolism and in which (where present) the concept of a metaphysical paradisiacal realm is a perfected, idyllic nature rather than a designed garden. It has also shown that gardens are made around Indian Hindu temples and that by and large these are places of horticultural cultivation rather than works of garden art. And while Balinese *pura* design included gardens with both a metaphorical symbolism and a dramatic aesthetic they are not an earthly expression of an otherworldly paradise. We have also identified that the Aztec cosmos possessed two paradisiacal realms: Tamoanchan, home of the gods and location of the creation myth, and Tlalocan, an especially delightful and exclusive afterlife. From their descriptions both can be considered a perfected nature with garden art overtones rather than a divinely-inspired garden form. However, both provided inspiration for royal pleasure gardens made by Aztec kings, gardens which simultaneously had a religious significance

LEFT A seed head of *huautli*. The seeds were used both as a food source and in religious ceremonies and festivals.

and role. According to Patrizia Granziera in her article 'Concept of the garden in Pre-Hispanic Mexico' such gardens were created:

> on natural sacred places where the work of man in the form of canals, pools, temples, reliefs existed in perfect harmony with natural features such as mountains, caves and springs. This garden was not only a representation of a terrestrial paradise, a Tlalocan-Tamoanchan, but also it was a ritual place where kings and magnates performed rites that linked their people to the sacred forces of the earth and sky that gave them life.

The fifteenth-century hilltop gardens of the poet-king Nezahualcoyotl (1402–72) of the Acolhua at Texcoco were deliberately sited at Tetzcotzingo, a space sacred to Tlaloc and were described in the seventeenth century by the native chronicler Fernando de Alva Cortés Ixtlilxóchitl (born between 1568 and 1580–1648).

> These parks and gardens were adorned with rich and sumptuously ornamented alcazars [summerhouses] with their fountains, their irrigation channels, their canals, their lakes and their bathing-places and wonderful mazes, where he had had a great variety of flowers planted and trees of all kinds, foreign and brought from distant parts [i.e this was also a botanic garden] … and the water intended for the fountains, pools and channels for watering the flowers and trees in this park came from its spring: to bring it, it had been necessary to build

strong, high, cemented walls of unbelievable size, going from one mountain to the other with an aqueduct on top which came out at the highest part of the park.

It has recently been ascertained that the gardens were carefully aligned with astronomical events, especially those associated with the planet Venus, and not as previously assumed simply along cardinal directions.

Not to be outdone the Mexican ruler Montezuma I (c.1398–1469) created the spectacular garden of Huaxtepec which is now sadly beneath a water theme park and holiday resort. Set among mountains and hills, crossed by a river which has its spring in the garden, with a cave nearby and boasting three natural bodies of water the garden's very location was a natural sacred site and very possibly representational of Tlalocan. Integrated among these natural features the artfully designed works of man in the form of canals, pools, temples and plants coexisted in perfect harmony. The result was a delightful garden full of sensory gratification, but one which was simultaneously layered and complex. Food crops were supplied to the royal household in the form of tribute and edible plants were excluded. Instead, Huaxtepec became renowned for its extensive botanical collection and in particular its medicinal plants. Just as with Mesopotamian *pairidaēza* and ancient Chinese hunting parks this vast collection brought from all corners of the king's empire demonstrated both its extent and his power. The latter was underscored by the prominence given in the garden to a series of carved relief statues depicting and celebrating the

LEFT An illustration in the sixteenth-century Tovar Codex showing Montezuma I, creator of Huaxtepec, receiving a crown.

OPPOSITE A map of Huaxtepec from *Pintura de Huaxtepec* (c.1580). The building in the centre is the Convento de Santo Domingo.

king's ancestors. And confirming his position at the head of the priesthood the king performed sacred ceremonies in the garden, the rituals of which would have made use of the ornamental, aromatic and medicinal plants grown there. It is also interesting to note that after planting trees gardeners performed a ritualistic autosacrifice - piercing their upper ears and sprinkling their blood on the soil before fasting for eight days. The deities worshipped here were mostly related to fertility, procreation, dancing and singing, while Matlacxochitl, a kind of goddess of medicine, confirmed the importance of Huaxtepec as a physic garden. Thus the garden was at once a cosmic paradigm, an important religious centre, a scientific botanic garden and a place of beauty and pleasure where artistic performances were held.

Finally, here is a description of Huaxtepec made by the Spanish scholar Francisco Cervantes de Salazar (1514?–1575). In a chapter of his *Crónica de Nueva España* (c.1565 but unpublished until the nineteenth century) entitled 'Of the gardens which Montezuma went for recreation', he reports as follows:

This great monarch had many pleasances and spacious gardens with paths and channels for irrigation. These gardens contained only medicinal and aromatic herbs, flowers, native roses, and trees with fragrant blossoms, of which there are many kinds. He ordered his physicians to make experiments with the medicinal herbs and to employ those best known and tried as remedies in healing the diseases of the lords of his court. These gardens gave great pleasures to all who visited them on account of the flower and roses they contained and of the fragrances they gave forth, especially in the mornings and evenings. It was well worth seeing with how much art and delicacy a thousand figures of persons were made by means of leaves and flowers, also seats, chapels, and the other constructions which so greatly adorned these places. In this flower garden Montezuma did not allow any vegetables or fruit to be grown, saying that it was not kingly to cultivate plants for utility or profit in his pleasance. He said that vegetable gardens and orchards were for slaves or merchants. At the same time he owned such, but they were far away and he seldom visited them.

# Texcotzingo
## Mexico City, Mexico

In 1431 after over a decade in exile and a three-year military campaign Nezahualcoyotl (1402–72) a philosopher, poet, architect and warrior, finally reconquered his heritage and was named ruler of the city state of Texcoco. The city was on the eastern bank of Lake Texcoco some 32 kilometres (20 miles) northeast of the Aztec capital Tenochtitlan. On a hill five kilometres (3 miles) to the west of Texcoco Nezahualcoyotl had made the royal summer palace and garden complex of Texcotzingo. Today both the city and palace lie within the greater metropolitan area of Mexico City, and the archaeological site of Texcotzingo provides an insight into both their former grandeur and ingenuity of design. An especially good example of the latter were the feats of hydraulic engineering that watered both the complex and the farm land at the foot of the hill, and which included an eight-kilometre (5-mile) long aqueduct that in places rose to 61 metres (200 feet).

Within the series of garden terraces created around the hillside water was a major theme. It filled bathing pools that were cut into the bedrock and which were as ornamental as they were practical; it fed fountains and waterfalls that cascaded down flights of stone steps, and it greened a barren hillside. Indeed, by making Texcotzingo a well-watered hill Nezahualcoyotl created a living embodiment of *altépetl*, a Nahuatl word formed of the words meaning 'hill' and 'water' that encapsulated the essence of the city state. Thus the garden possessed a dynastic/ancestral symbolism and was a monument to his power.

Like Huaxtepec and also in another display of power gardening, Texcotzingo also boasted an extensive botanical collection of plants. But here the plants that provided the Aztecs with food security were also grown: maize, beans and squash – plants which themselves were considered gods-given. But the religio-symbolism ran deeper than merely growing revered plants. Again like Huaxtepec this garden was a paradisiacal landscape dedicated to the rain god Tlaloc and an earthly imitation of Tlalocan. Monolithic sculptures and symbolic representations were set throughout to emphasise the garden's mythical significance but here the hand of man was more necessary for the creation of an earthly paradise on a barren hillside than it was in the naturally blessed location chosen by Montezuma.

OPPOSITE AND RIGHT
Although now dry, the remains of the canal system, cascades, fountains and pools that once enlivened the gardens give an indication both of how significant water was to these symbolic gardens and what an engineering achievement it was to deliver water to them.

OVERLEAF
A panorama of the archaeological site that today is Tetzcotzingo shows the prominence that the hilltop location had in relation to its immediate surroundings and offers an indication of the impressive scale of the gardens that once graced this summer palace.

# New beliefs

So far this book has looked at the symbolic role of plants and divine gardens in ancient and current belief systems, and how such gardens have influenced earthly garden design. For millions of believers around the world divine nature, symbolic plants and religio-gardens continue to be a meaningful and inspirational component of their religion and, as will be seen, in some cases there have been contemporary developments. However, this final chapter also examines how plants and gardens continue to play a large cultural and emotional role in contemporary secular society and how gardens today provide important psychological and health-giving benefits.

In 1932 and in a new variation on an old theme the Virgin Mary became associated with a Mary Garden when the first publicly accessible example was made at St Joseph's Church in Wood's Hole, Massachusetts. The modern Mary Garden may be of any size but its form features a centrally positioned statue of the Virgin Mary surrounded by plants that have a Mary symbolism or connection. About eight hundred such plants have been identified and while some have a direct biblical link, for example, in the Song of Solomon Mary says: 'I am the Rose of Sharon' [possibly *Pancratium maritimum*], the lily of the valleys' [sometimes identified as *Anemone coronaria*], for others the association is tenuous, as in the Star of Bethlehem (*Campanula isophylla*). A full list of Mary plants is available online from the Marian Library of the International Marian Research Institute at the University of Dayton, Ohio.

A few of the about eight hundred plants that are today considered as having an association with the Virgin Mary. The lily of the valley (*Convallaria majalis*, opposite) is also known as Mary's tears. The strawberry (top right) is symbolic of Mary as the fruitful virgin. Mary became associated with the 'rose of Sharon', another possible candidate for which is the sea daffodil (second down) through a verse in the Song of Solomon. The hawthorn (third down) became known as Mary's Flower of May, while Saint Bernard compared her virginity to a white rose (bottom) and her charity to a red one.

PARADISE GARDENS

Making use of urban greenspace improves the health of city residents. Additional less obvious but equally significant benefits have been generated by the Aga Khan Trust for Culture which has created Al-Azhar Park (left), thirty new hectares of much-needed and Islamic-inspired greenspace in Cairo and restored the historic *chahar bagh* gardens of Humayun's tomb in Delhi (below).

Even more recently, the creation of the new, Islamic-inspired Al-Azhar public park in Cairo funded by His Royal Highness the Aga Khan IV and the restoration of the historic gardens surrounding Humayun's tomb in Delhi, both of which were undertaken by the Aga Khan Trust for Culture, have established a new paradigm. Not only are urban residents of these two bustling and crowded cities now provided with much-needed recreational green space but the gardens are also a catalyst for urban rehabilitation. The physical, social and economic infrastructure of the adjacent (and in both cases very poor) neighbourhoods have been substantially ameliorated through a combination of housing renovations, health, education and skills training programmes and microcredit schemes.

And just as the Islamic garden can trace its origins to Persia so too can the delightful formal garden that provides the setting for the domed Shrine of the Báb, one of the most holy shrines and sacred pilgrimage sites of the Bahá'í faith which was founded in 1844 by Bahá'u'lláh (the Báb). Created between 1990 and 2001 nineteen terraces (eighteen garden terraces plus one for the shrine) are linked by a set of steps flanked by twin streams that cascade almost a kilometre (about half a mile) down the northern slope of Mount Carmel in Haifa, Israel. The eighteen garden terraces symbolise the Letter of the Living or the first eighteen disciples of the Báb, and while the garden may be considered a visual symbol of the Baha'i, emphasis on worldwide religious unity

is not strictly an earthly expression of a divine paradise. Nevertheless gardens are significant within the faith for Bahá'u'lláh resided in the Najibiyyih Garden in Baghdad, Iraq, during the period when he declared his prophetic mission to his followers in 1863. Bahá'u'lláh called the garden Ridván, meaning paradise, and thus the garden is commemorated in the festival of the same name which celebrates Bahá'u'lláh's pronouncement. Garden allegory is also used by Bahá'u'lláh in his writings, for instance when describing the 'fruits of communion' with God in the garden of the heart in *The Seven Valleys and the Four Valleys* he lyrically wrote, 'wert thou to taste of these fruits, from the green garden of these blossoms which grow in the lands of knowledge'.

Made in eleven years from 1990, a garden of eighteen terraces with associated planting and water features was built on the side of Mount Carmel in Haifa, Israel in order to create a magnificent setting for the golden-domed Shrine of the Báb, a destination of sacred pilgrimage for members of the Bahá'í faith.

PARADISE GARDENS

# The Woodland Cemetery
## Stockholm, Sweden

In 1912 an international competition was held for a new cemetery on 96 hectares of disused gravel quarry and pine forest overgrown with pine trees in Enskede in the southern part of Stockholm. The competition was won by two young Swedish architects, Gunnar Asplund and Sigurd Lewerentz who found inspiration not from the then fashionable modernism but by reworking with an old-fashioned sentimentalism traditional elements of Pagan and medieval Nordic burial archetypes. The Nordic was combined with skilful use of, and subtle references to literature and buildings from Mediterranean antiquity — for example, the Via Sepulchra at Pompeii. The result is an extraordinarily poignant landscape and an outstandingly successful example of a designed cultural landscape; the sympathetic, considered and empathic shaping of nature with its integral buildings resulting in an atmosphere of tranquil beauty.

Although consecrated as a Lutheran cemetery the symbolism of the architecture and landscape is all the more affecting and powerful precisely because it is not intended to appeal to any one faith or any one time. Dignity and no undue alteration of the existing landscape — a key demand of the competition design brief — are found in the shallow pond and outdoor catafalque surrounded by blazing braziers in front of the Chapel of the Holy Cross and the crooked trees on the top of the hill behind them. Lewerentz was principally responsible for the radical landscape design which evokes a primitive imagery of raw

Nordic wilderness conjoined with an intense romantic naturalism; and by hiding the crematorium underground he simultaneously created significant settings for the chapels above. The graves themselves are laid out without excessive alignment or regimentation among the natural forest and the impact of footpaths, meandering freely through the woodland, is minimal. The landscape is also deeply in tune with the mourners' experience, that is, the feelings associated with loss. The processional routes leading to the chapels are designed to create the appropriate mood prior to the funeral service, while afterwards, attention is drawn to the natural surroundings, to help reconcile the mourners with their sadness and to introduce hope in the theme of nature's cycles of birth, death and rebirth.

The woodland setting for the graves generates a strong bond between living nature and the memorial to the deceased. This closeness makes visiting the grave of a loved one a very emotional yet calming experience.

The architecture is in complete sympathy and harmony with its landscape setting and the lake acting as a mirror on a still day creates an ethereal link between the earth and the heavens it reflects.

The variable Swedish climate strongly influences the atmosphere and the visual experience of Skogskyrkogården, be this on an hourly, daily or seasonal timeframe. Nevertheless emotional response to the Almhöjden (or meditation grove) is intended to be one of reflection and remembrance.

In today's world plants are widely used as emblems to declare identity as well as to identify political office and institutions. The Welsh have their leek, the Scots their thistle, the Irish their shamrock and the English their rose, while the flags of Canada and Lebanon depict a maple leaf and a cedar of Lebanon tree respectively. The olive as a symbol of peace appears both grasped in the right talon of the bald eagle on the seal of the President of the United States and on the flag and emblem of the United Nations. Simultaneously, for secular members of society many plants have lost their sacro-religious symbolism yet continue to play an important role in their lives. We have seen how the Christmas tree became established as the customary decoration of the festive period and many people also ornament their home with daffodils (*Narcissus* spp.) at Easter as well as giving red roses to their beloved on 14 February, the feast day of Saint Valentine. A little more obscure is the celebration on 31 October of Hallowe'en. The name is a contraction of All Hallows' Eve which is part of Hallowtide, the triduum which includes All Saints' Day (1 November) and All Souls' Day (2 November) and is a time of remembering the dead – especially saints,

martyrs and relatives. The Romans celebrated Pomona, the goddess of fruit in October, but with its origins dating to the fifth century it is likely that Hallowe'en was an example of syncretism involving the Celtic festival of Samhain which marked the end of the harvest and the beginning of the darker months. Today the symbol of Hallowe'en is the pumpkin whose lit candles have a faint echo of the fire rituals of Samhain. Lanterns were carried by guisers on All Hallows' Eve in order to frighten away evil spirits but the jack-o'-lantern evolved in Ireland from a folktale involving a soul refused entry into both heaven and hell. When he was alive Jack tricked Satan into climbing a tree and then carved a cross in the tree's trunk thus trapping the devil. Striking a bargain that the devil would never tempt him again, Jack released him. Upon his death Jack was refused entry into heaven on account of his wayward life and Satan in revenge refused him entry into hell and threw a glowing coal at Jack's soul. This

ABOVE Devon and Somerset apple growers wassail orchards in January with songs and a bucket of hot cider. This illustration from 1913 shows a libation being splashed on a tree, after which the wassailers will drink the rest of the brew.

LEFT A greetings card depicting a jack-o'-lantern. The celebration of All Hallows' Eve has seen a revival in recent years although the religious symbolism has all but been forgotten.

Jack placed in a hollowed-out turnip to keep it burning and used it as a light in his endless searching for a place to rest. The jack-o'-lantern was taken to America in the 1840s by émigrés from the famine who quickly adopted the larger pumpkin as a more expedient vessel; now the tradition has been re-exported back to Europe. One last example of plant symbolism of religious origin that has become commonplace is the bouquet that brides still toss over their shoulders (the one who catches it will be the next to wed). This is a vestige of a fourteenth-century belief that brides were especially auspicious and that a piece of their wedding dress would bring good luck. Rather than have their dress cut from them brides began to carry and dispense flowers, which were also symbolic of a bride's status as a maid in bloom.

Contemporary culture has also seen the rise of new beliefs including neopaganism, a group of modern faiths influenced by or claiming derivation from the various historical pagan belief systems among which nature-reverence, animism, pantheism and polytheism are commonly found. Older pagan traditions that have experienced a resurgence in recent

BELOW The tradition of wassailing held in an orchard on the edge of Kenninghall Wood in Norfolk includes other revived pagan traditions with both the green man and the Lord of Misrule trying to wake the spirits of the trees from the depths of winter.

decades include hanging mistletoe from a door frame at Christmas time – the tradition of kissing beneath it traces its origins back to Frijjō (Frigg) the Norse goddess of love. In the cider producing areas of England people once again go wassailing. The word 'wassail' derives from the Anglo-Saxon toast '*Wæs þu hæl*' meaning 'be you in good health' and in a melding of pagan and Christian customs it is conducted on Twelfth night, which, according to the *Shorter Oxford English Dictionary* is 'the night of the twelfth day after Christmas (6 January) marked by merrymaking'. The exact ceremony varies from area to area but in general a procession led by the wassail king and queen progresses from apple orchard to apple orchard and in each one the congregation sing and make incantations to the trees, for example:

> 'Here's to thee, old apple tree,
> That blooms well, bears well,
> Hats full, caps full,
> Three bushel bags full,
> An' all under one tree.
> Hurrah! Hurrah!'

The trees are toasted in cider and/or libations are poured after which the assembled crowd makes an unholy racket by banging drums and pots and pans. The aim is to awaken the

LEFT A beautiful example of well dressing from the village
of Tissington in Derbyshire where it is believed the tradition
began in 1349. Today the annual well dressing ceremony
takes place on Ascension Day.

May through to August. Wooden boards are soaked in water
for several days before being covered with a layer of wet clay
on which the design is marked and coloured in using flower
petals, and later in the season, seeds. A calendar of dressings
can be found on the welldressing website.

Another pre-Christian celebration that underwent
syncretism and continues to be enjoyed is May Day. Now also
associated with International Workers' Day, it can trace its
origins to the Celtic festival of Beltane and the Roman festival
of Floralia, both of which were held at the end of April to
herald the beginning of summer. In the former case houses,
byres and livestock were decorated with mayweed (*Anthemis
arvensis*), whose yellow flower may have symbolised the
sacred fire so central to the rituals, while in parts of Ireland
villagers would also make a May bush. A cut branch of
hawthorn (*Crataegus monogyna*, also known as May tree) was
set in the ground (outside, never indoors) and decorated with
wild flowers. In eighth century Germany the Celtic tradition
became Walpurgis Night, the eve of the feast day of Saint
Walpurga (she is credited with bringing Christianity to the
country) which subsequently became associated with May
Day, especially in Scandinavia. Today's celebrations follow
tradition with a parade led by the May Queen crowned with
flowers and whose persona is possibly a relic of tree worship.
The May Queen also leads the dancing around the maypole,
traditionally a tall tree trunk with ribbons attached to it,
whose symbolism may also be associated with tree worship
and the *axis mundi*.

In our modern world there are also plants and garden
types with no religious connection that strike an emotional
chord and which can positively affect the mental and physical
health of believer and non-believer alike. Floriography or
cryptological communication by means of flowers was used by
Shakespeare who ascribed emblematic meanings to plants in
several of his works including *Hamlet* when Ophelia exclaims:
'There's rosemary, that's for remembrance. Pray you, love,
remember. And there is pansies, that's for thoughts.' Its
origins are older still (an example is the Song of Solomon) but
it was in Victorian Britain that floriography reached its zenith.

tree for the forthcoming spring and to scare away evil spirits
in order to ensure a successful harvest in the coming year.

Just as the sacred oak provided a doorway to the otherworld so the Celts also believed that springs were another
portal into this realm. It is generally accepted that the custom
of well dressing for which the Peak District of Derbyshire
and Staffordshire is most famous originated as some form
of Celtic veneration of spring deities. This practice was
suppressed by the early Church but revived in 1349 by the
residents in the village of Tissington when they gave thanks
for avoiding the Black Death. Their deliverance they believed
was due to the fact the villagers had only drunk of the spring
water. The practice of ornamenting wells and springs with
pictures made from flower petals has waxed and waned down
the centuries but in recent decades its popularity has been
on the rise and has spread to other parts of England. The
dressings – which can involve up to a week's work to make
and then only last about the same time – take place from

Using texts such as *The Language of Flowers* (1857) it became fashionable to communicate through a gift of flowers, a plant or a bouquet those feelings and emotions which in that repressed society could not be spoken aloud. Of course certain flowers still deliver a message, white lilies for instance signify mourning, but who now knows that this flower once meant 'sweetness, virginity, purity, majesty and it is heavenly to be with you'? Similarly a red rose today declares 'I love you' but it once meant 'passion' while a yellow rose meant 'infidelity', a pink one 'happiness' and a white one, perhaps not surprisingly, 'purity'. According to *The Language of Flowers* the sentiment represented by the red poppy was, appropriately, 'consolation' for today it means, 'we remember'. First adopted by the American Legion in 1920 as a symbol to commemorate those soldiers who had fallen during the Great War the Remembrance Poppy was similarly adopted by the Royal British Legion and Commonwealth veterans groups the following year. Its use was inspired by the war poem 'In Flanders Fields' written in 1915 by Canadian physician Lieutenant Colonel John McCrae which makes references to wild red poppies (*Papaver rhoeas*) growing on the graves of dead soldiers.

ABOVE A charming postcard from the Victorian period showing young girls in white dresses dancing around a maypole. The long streamers they hold are woven into a pattern around the pole as they dance.

BELOW This vintage postcard gave the recipient a lesson in the language of flowers. Note that as for the Virgin Mary the violet symbolises modesty.

OVERLEAF 'Blood Swept Lands and Seas of Red' was a moving art installation created by artists Paul Cummins and Tom Piper at the Tower of London in 2014 to commemorate the outbreak of the First World War. Precisely 888,246 ceramic poppies progressively filled the Tower's moat, one for every British and Commonwealth soldier who died.

The language of flowers

Cornflower Riches
Daisy Attachment
Hundred leaved Rose Sincere love
Violet Modesty
Convolvulus Tender love
Heather Solitude

Geranium Sincerity
Nettle Defiance
Lily of the valley Sensitiveness
Yellow Rose Contentment
Rhododendron Strength
Narcissus Pride

Jasmine Faithfulness
Gentian Gratitude
Edelweiss Cleanliness
Pansy Messenger of love
White rose Purity
Pink Hope

# Leichtag Family Healing Garden
## San Diego, USA

In her own words the landscape architect Topher Delaney 'made a pact with God' that if she survived her breast cancer she would make a garden for other patients to enjoy. Both sides kept their bargain and at the Marin General Hospital's outpatient medical building in California Delaney transformed a small, unused space into a meditation garden. A strong believer in the power of a garden to have dramatically positive influences on its users, especially those experiencing illness and stress, Delaney designed a healing garden with flowers and fountains that can also be seen from within the oncology department. This was the first of several such gardens she has made, including the Leichtag Family Healing Garden at the Rady Children's Hospital in San Diego. In contrast to the tranquillity of a meditation garden a children's hospital garden needs to be an environment that offers a respite from medical care while providing stimulation for play and an outlet for

If the wind blows hard enough the blades of the Rainbow Windmill glow white.

LEFT Bright colours dominate the garden making for a cheerful space in which patients and their families can seek solace and respite.

ABOVE The Constellation Wall lights up at night with the twelve signs of the zodiac.

enthusiasm and activity; yet it must also provide a place where children can relax and be with their families.

The hospital's website states that the concept of this healing garden is 'rooted in our commitment to consistently nourish the physical, emotional, mental and spiritual needs of children, their families and our staff through our healing environment. Our wish is that when visitors leave the garden, they will feel strengthened and renewed.' To this end the garden provides a retreat and a haven and is a deliberate distraction from and strong contrast with the clinical atmosphere of the hospital's interior. One enters the garden between the

legs of a six-metre (20-foot) tall brontosaurus and once inside bright colours cover the floors and walls, while a tile-covered two-metre (6½-foot) tall seahorse fountain squirts water into a raised pool and a rainbow-coloured windmill spins. If the wind is strong enough the coloured blades glow white. Shaded benches can be wheeled around this cheerful space and as night falls the Constellation Wall lights up with the twelve signs of the zodiac. This is most definitely a positive place which through play and exploration or just by being there provides an uplifting interlude in an otherwise difficult time.

Certain narcotic plants which are now illegal or considered pernicious have a long history of religious use, and even now are manipulated for political ends. Cannabis (*Cannabis sativa*) has been used widely as an entheogen by cultures as far back as about 1500 BCE. It is one of the five sacred plants named in the Atharvaveda, which dates to c.1200–1000 BCE and became one of the four sacred texts of Hinduism. It was used by Taoists and Herodotus described how Scythians took cannabis steam baths. It was associated with the Norse love goddess, Frijjō and the Rastafari spiritual movement, which arose in the 1930s, used cannabis as part of the worship of their king Haile Selassie I.

In recent years the debate over the therapeutic benefits of cannabis has heated up while tobacco, used for thousands of years in sacred ceremony by so many pre-Columbian peoples has been vilified and cited in several class action suits against tobacco companies running into the billions of dollars. Yet ironically the tobacco plant itself is now being heralded in the medical world as a successful vehicle for the biosynthetic production of drugs, for example the anti-malarial Artemisinin.

More injurious still is opium, the dried latex extracted from the opium poppy, which was used entheogenically by the Minoans, in the Eleusinian Mysteries by ancient Greeks and was widely smoked by Muslims as an alternative to drinking alcohol which the Qu'ran forbids. Ending the Afghan opium trade was a key argument used in 2001 by the then prime minister Tony Blair to justify deploying British troops to the country, since when the annual opium harvest has done nothing but increase to (excuse the pun) an UNODC-estimated high of 5,500 tons in 2013. But to put this figure in perspective it is a paltry fourteen per cent of the 39,000 tons of Indian-produced opium the British Government sold annually to China at the turn of the twentieth century.

The conflict in Afghanistan has also provided examples of what landscape architect Kenneth Helphand terms 'Defiant Gardens'. Such gardens are made 'in extreme or difficult environmental, social, political, economic, or cultural conditions' and other war-torn locations where Defiant Gardens have been made include the trenches of the First World War, Warsaw and other ghettos under Nazi suppression together with prisoner-of-war and internment camps in Europe, the United States and Asia during the Second World War. Defiant Gardens represent 'adaptation to challenging circumstances' and hope – islands of beauty and calm in a sea of ugliness, fear and chaos. In circumstances where death is all around sowing seed is a positive, optimistic act of living while gardening itself has a beneficial psychological impact by reducing stress, improving mental clarity and increasing emotional well-being. Moreover, a garden planted with familiar flowers and vegetables in a foreign land reaffirms one's personal and cultural identity and acts as a reminder of and link with 'back home'.

Gardening, or more specifically horticulture therapy (also called social and therapeutic horticulture), has been demonstrated to have a significant positive impact in assisting the rehabilitation of wounded veterans, both those who have suffered physical injury and those with psychological traumas such as post-traumatic stress disorder. Defined by the American Horticultural Therapy Association as 'a process utilising plants and horticultural activities to improve social, educational, psychological and physical adjustment of persons thus improving their body, mind, and spirit', horticulture therapy can also bring about many positive changes in the lives of those living with ill-health or a disability, as well as those who are vulnerable, isolated or disadvantaged. Such therapy is often engaged in within a therapeutic garden which may be created in a variety of healthcare and residential environments including hospitals, skilled nursing homes, assisted living residences, out-patient cancer centres and hospices. Carefully designed as a space that offers sensory stimulation and as an arena for social interaction and recreation, a therapeutic garden meets the physical, psychological, social and spiritual needs of users, their caregivers, family and friends. In terms of health benefits, the positive and safe

psychological environment reduces stress levels and so aids recovery as well as stimulating the benefits mentioned above, while participating in the act of gardening also has physiological benefits such as training both cognitive and sensory-motor functions.

But the well-being benefits of green space are not restricted to therapeutic gardens. Study after study has shown that for urban dwellers simply being in their own garden or a public park has numerous health and social benefits. Green space can be a tranquil haven that offers solace from busy, stressful lives while fostering active living can help in combating sedentary lifestyle diseases associated with obesity, including diabetes, heart disease and several types of cancer. Moreover, given the choice, most children would prefer to play in outdoor spaces. Such activities as well as keeping children fit and healthy provide them with a range of sensory experiences and help them to refine their motor skills. Community gardens, which have become a recent feature of many inner city parks give residents space for social and intercultural interaction and may also foster closer community ties while enabling people to supplement their diets with fresh fruit and vegetables. Last but not least, at an environmental level urban parks and gardens provide many benefits including improving air quality, reducing noise, sequestering carbon and increasing biodiversity.

And of course green spaces offer an opportunity to indulge in the latest form of arboreal veneration — tree hugging. It has never been so popular, and for those wishing to give it a try here are some instructions and variations on the theme:

1. Find a quiet park or wooded area.

2. Walk among the trees until you feel comfortable.

3. Feel the different textures of bark with the palms of your hands.

4. Inhale the scent of the different trees.

5. Look upwards through the spreading branches.

6. Find the tree that fits your mood.

## Vertical Tree Hug

Encircle the trunk with your arms while gently pressing your cheek to the trunk (taking care not to scratch your face). Hold tightly, breathe deeply and be one with your tree.

## Full Body Tree Hug

Sit upon the ground wrapping your legs around the base of the tree and at the same time embracing it with your arms. Hold tightly, breathe deeply and be one with your tree.

## Up in the Air Tree Hug

This is only for the athletic. Climb your tree and straddle a strong branch. Bend forward and place your belly against it while wrapping your arms about it. Hold tightly, breathe deeply and be one with your tree.

Enjoy — and remember to thank the tree afterwards!

Trees may … or may not link the underworld, the earth and the heavens, but certainly they are intrinsic to all belief systems and are beautiful in and of themselves.

OVERLEAF Sunset over Rocky Mountain National Park in Colorado, USA. Our earliest ancestors worshipped nature and since then many religions have venerated 'him' or, more usually, 'her'. Today we understand much of the science of nature yet at a subconscious psychological level we continue to react positively to beautiful scenes such as this.

For so many thousands of years all major belief systems the world over have commanded that nature, plants and gardens are a positive gift to us from the god(s) or the supernatural forces that bind the universe together. And as a species, regardless of ethnicity, geography or chronology, and whether or not we are believers, we are truly blessed. Blessed because we humans can and do positively respond to the many delights and benefits that nature, plants and gardens bring and give us. Today, paradise gardens may be an earthly expression of the divinely prescribed, a meditative tool to aid an inner discovery or, for the secular, an expression of creativity, a personal haven. Whatever the inspiration, the purpose of a plant-filled garden is the same: to make us better as people and thus collectively, and hopefully, as a society.

Miniature of the Creation, from Paulus Orosius,
*Histoire Ancienne*, France, c.1415

# Bibliography

GENERAL TEXTS

Cleene, M. & LeJeune, M.C., *Compendium of Symbolic and Ritual Plants in Europe*, vols I & II (2003), Mens & Cultuur Uitgevers n.v.

Gothein, M-L. (trans. Archer-Hind, L., ed. Wright, W.P.), *A History of Garden Art*, vols I & II (1928). J.M. Dent & Sons.

Hobhouse, P., *The Story of Gardening* (2002), Dorling Kindersley.

Rodgers, E., *Landscape Design* (2001), Harry N Abrams.

## Classical and ancient belief systems

EGYPT

Baumann, B.B., 'The Botanical Aspects of Ancient Egyptian Embalming and Burial', *Economic Botany*, 14:1 (Jan–Mar 1960), pp.84–104.

Carroll, M., *Earthly Paradises: Ancient Gardens in History and Archaeology* (2003), British Museum Press.

Wilkinson, A., 'Symbolism and Design in Ancient Egyptian Gardens', *Garden History*, 22:1 (Summer 1994), pp.1–17.

Wilkinson, A., *The Garden in Ancient Egypt* (1998), London, p.130.

MINOAN

Cain, C.D., 'Dancing in the Dark: Deconstructing a Narrative of Epiphany on the Isopata Ring', *American Journal of Archaeology*, 105:1 (Jan 2001), pp.27–49.

Chapin, A.P., 'Power, Privilege, and Landscape in Minoan Art', *Hesperia Supplements*, 33 XAPIΣ: Essays in Honor of Sara A. Immerwahr (2004), pp.47–64.

Dietrich, B.C., 'Death and Afterlife in Minoan Religion', *Kernos*, 10 (1997), pp.19–38.

Evans, A., '"The Ring of Nestor" : A Glimpse into the Minoan After-World and A Sepulchral Treasure of Gold Signet-Rings and Bead-Seals from Thisbê, Boeotia', *The Journal of Hellenic Studies*, 45:1 (1925), pp.1–75.

Herva, V-P., 'Flower Lovers, after All? Rethinking Religion and Human-Environment Relations in MinoanCrete'. *World Archaeology*, 38:4 *Debates in 'World Archaeology'* (Dec 2006), pp.586–598.

Huebner, K., 'The Sanctuary Rhyton', *Anistoriton*, 7 (2003), p.32. http://corescholar.libraries.wright.edu/art/2

Mlynarczyk, J., *Report of the Department of Antiquities Cyprus* (1980), p.244.

Mlynarczyk, J., *Report of the Department of Antiquities Cyprus* (1985), p.286.

Rhizopoulou, S., 'Symbolic plant(s) of the Olympic Games', *Journal of Experimental Botany*, 55:403 (Aug 2004), pp.1601–1606.

Semple, E.C., 'Ancient Mediterranean Pleasure Gardens', *Geographical Review*, 19:3 (July 1929), pp.420–443.

Shaw, M.C., 'The Aegean Garden', *American Journal of Archaeology*, 97:4 (Oct 1993), pp. 661–685.

Simms, R.R., 'Mourning and Community at the Athenian Adonia', *The Classical Journal*, 93:2 (Dec 1997–Jan 1998), pp.121–141.

MESOPOTAMIAN

Albenda, P., 'Assyrian Sacred Trees in the Brooklyn Museum', *Iraq*, 56 (1994), pp.123–133.

Botta, P.E. and Flandin, E., *Monument de Ninive*, vol. 2 (1849), Imprimerie Nationale.

ed. Devlin-Glass, F., *Feminist Poetics of the Sacred: Creative Suspicions* (2001), Oxford University Press, pp.91–103.

Katz, D., 'Enki and Ninhursağa, Part One: The Story of Dilmun', *Bibliotheca Orientalis*, LXIV N° 5–6, (Sept–Dec, 2007). pp.568–586.

Lechler, G., The Tree of Life in Indo-European and Islamic Cultures. *Ars Islamica*, 4 (1937), pp.369–419.

Luckenbill, D.D., *Ancient Records of Assyria and Babylon*, vol. I (1926), University of Chicago Press, pp.174–75

Parpola, S., 'The Assyrian Tree of Life: Tracing the Origins of Jewish Monotheism and Greek Philosophy' *Journal of Near Eastern Studies*, 52: 3 (July, 1993), pp.161–208.

Simo, P., 'The Assyrian Tree of Life: Tracing the Origins of Jewish Monotheism and Greek Philosophy', *Journal of Near Eastern Studies*, 52:3 (July, 1993), pp.161–208.

Stager, L.E., 'Jerusalem as Eden', *Biblical Archaeology Review*, 26:3 (2000), pp.31 & 48.

Wiseman, D.J., 'Mesopotamian Gardens', *Anatolian Studies*, 33 Special Number in Honour of the Seventy-Fifth Birthday of Dr. Richard Barnett (1983), pp.137–144.

GREECE

Mlynarczyk, J., *Report of the Department of Antiquities Cyprus* (1980), p. 244.

Mlynarczyk, J., *Report of the Department of Antiquities Cyprus* (1985), p. 286.

Rhizopoulou, S., 'Symbolic plant(s) of the Olympic Games', *Journal of Experimental Botany*, 55:403 (Aug 2004), pp.1601–1606.

Shaw, M.C., 'The Aegean Garden', *American Journal of Archaeology*, 97:4 (Oct 1993), pp.661–685.

Simms, R.R., 'Mourning and Community at the Athenian Adonia', *The Classical Journal*, 93:2 (Dec 1997–Jan 1998), pp.121–141.

ROMAN

Farrar, L., *Ancient Roman Gardens* (1998), Sutton Publishing Ltd.

Jashemski, W.F., Foss, J.E., Lewis, R.J., Timpson, M.E., Lee, S.Y., 'Roman Gardens in Tunisia: Preliminary Excavations in the House of Bacchus and Ariadne and in the East Temple at Thuburbo Maius', *American Journal of Archaeology*, 99:4 (Oct 1995), pp.559–576.

Lawson, J., 'The Roman Garden', *Greece & Rome*, 19:57 (Oct 1950), pp.97–105.

Meyer, F.G., 'Carbonized Food Plants of Pompeii, Herculaneum, and the Villa at Torre Annunziata', *Economic Botany*, 34:4 (Oct–Dec 1980), pp.401–437.

# Abrahamic religions

### JUDAEO-CHRISTIAN

Comito, T., 'Renaissance Gardens and the Discovery of Paradise', *Journal of the History of Ideas*, 32:4 (Oct–Dec 1971), pp.483–506.

Delumeau, J., *History of Paradise: The Garden of Eden in Myth and Tradition* (new ed. 2000), University of Illinois Press.

Kosmer, E., 'Gardens of Virtue in the Middle Ages', *Journal of the Warburg and Courtauld Institutes*, 41 (1978), pp.302–307.

Harvey, J., *The Mediæval Garden* (1981), Batsford Ltd.

Landy, F., 'The Song of Songs and the Garden of Eden', *Journal of Biblical Literature*, 98:4 (Dec 1979), pp.513–528.

Trible, P., 'Depatriarchalizing in Biblical Interpretation', *Journal of the American Academy of Religion*, 41:1 (March 1973), pp.30–48.

### ISLAM

Clarke, E., *Underneath Which Rivers Flow* (1996), The Prince of Wales Institute of Architecture.

Dickie, J. (Yaqub Zaki), 'The Mughal Garden: Gateway to Paradise', *Muqarnas*, 3 (1985), pp.128–137.

Hamed, S.E-D., 'Paradise on earth: Historical gardens of the arid Middle East', *Aridlands Newsletter*, No. 36 (Fall/Winter 1994), University of Arizona. http://ag.arizona.edu/OALS/ALN/aln36/Hamed.html.

Harvey, J.H., 'Garden Plants of Moorish Spain: A Fresh Look', *Garden History*, 20:1 (Spring 1992), pp.71–82.

Koch, E., 'Mughal Palace Gardens from Babur to Shah Jahan (1526–1648)', *Muqarnas*, 14 (1997), pp.143–165.

ed. McDougall, E., *The Islamic Garden (Dumbarton Oaks Colloquium on the History of Landscape Architecture)* (1976), Dumbarton Oaks.

Moynihan, E.B., *Paradise as a Garden* (1982), Scolar Press.

Ruggles, D. Fairchild, *Islamic Gardens and Landscapes* (2008), University of Pennsylvania Press.

Wescoat, J.L. Jr., 'Mughal Gardens: The Re-emergence of Comparative Possibilities and the Wavering of Practical Concern', ed. Conan, M., *Perspectives on Garden Histories, Volume 21: History of Landscape Architecture Colloquium*, (1999), Dumbarton Oaks Research Library and Collection, pp.107–135.

# Eastern religions

### CHINA

Cooper, J., 'The Symbolism of the Taoist Garden', *Studies in Comparative Religion*, 11:4 (Autumn 1977).

Harrist, R.E., *Painting and Private Life in Eleventh-century China* (1998), Princeton University Press.

Hui Zou, *A Jesuit Garden in Beijing and Early Modern Chinese Culture* (2011), Purdue University Press.

Hunt, J.D., *A World of Gardens* (2012), Reaktion Books.

Keswick, M., *Chinese Gardens* (1978), Academy Editions, (new edition *The Chinese Garden*, ed Jencks, C. & Hardie, A. (2003) Frances Lincoln Ltd.

Koehn, A., 'Chinese Flower Symbolism', *Monumenta Nipponica*, 8:1/2 (1952), pp.121–146.

Li, H.L., *Garden Flowers of China* (1959), Ronald Press Co.

Prebish, C.S. & Keown, D., *Introducing Buddhism* (2009), Routledge, Taylor & Francis Group.

Pyysiäinen, I., 'Buddhism, Religion, and the Concept of "God"', *Numen*, 50:2 (2003), pp.147–171.

Rodgers, E. B., *Landscape Design* (2001), Harry H Abrams.

### JAPAN

Nitschke, G., *Japanese Gardens* (2003), Taschen.

Rodgers, E.B., *Landscape Design* (2001), Harry H Abrams.

trans. Seidensticker, E.G., *The Tale of Genji* (1980), Penguin.

trans. Takei, J. & Keane, M., *Sakuteiki* (2001), Tuttle Publishing.

Treib, M., *Guide to the Gardens of Kyoto* (2003), Kodansha International Ltd.

# Pantheism and polytheism

### HINDUISM

Gupta, S.M., *Plant Myths and Traditions in India* (2001), Munshirm Manoharlal.

Kramrisch, S., *The Hindu Temple* (1946), The University of Calcutta.

### EUROPEAN PAGANISM

ed. Chambers, E.K. & Sidgwick, F., *Early English Lyrics* (1926), B Blom.

Jones, P. & Pennick, N., *A History of Pagan Europe* (1995), Routledge.

Lehner, E. & I., *Folklore and Symbolism of Flowers, Plants and Trees* (2004), Dover Publications Inc.

Maclean, H., 'Gaelic Mythology',*The Journal of the Anthropological Institute of Great Britain and Ireland*, 9 (1880), pp.167–181.

ed. Monaghan, P., *Goddesses in World Culture*, vol. 1 (2011), Greenwood Press.

Monaghan, P., *The Encyclopedia of Celtic Mythology and Folklore* (2004), Infobase Publishing.

### NATIVE AMERICA

Brown, J.E., 'The Spiritual Legacy of the American Indian', *Studies in Comparative Religion*, 14:1–2. www.studiesincomparativereligion.com

Cornell, G., 'Native American Perceptions of the Environment', *Northeast Indian Quarterly*. VII: 2 (Summer 1990), pp.3–14.

Ford, R.I., 'Paleoethnobotany in American Archaeology', *Advances in Archaeological Method and Theory*, 2 (1979), pp.285–336.

Savinelli, A., *Plants of Power* (2002), Native Voices.

Stoffle, R.W., Halmo, D.B., Evans, M.J., Olmsted, J.E. 'Calculating the Cultural Significance of American Indian Plants: Paiute and Shoshone Ethnobotany at Yucca Mountain, Nevada', *American Anthropologist*, New Series, 92: 2 (June 1990), pp.416–432.

MESOAMERICA

Avilés, P., 'Seven Ways of Looking at a Mountain: Tetzcotzingo and the Aztec Garden Tradition', *Landscape Journal*, 25:2 (2006), pp.143–157.

Braakhuis, H.E.M., 'The Tonsured Maize God and Chicome-Xochitl as Maize Bringers and Culture Heroes: A Gulf Coast Perspective', *Wayeb Notes*, 32 (2009).

Caresco, D., *The Oxford Encyclopedia of Mesoamerican Cultures*, vols 1–3 (2000), Oxford University Press.

Evans, S.T., 'Aztec Royal Pleasure Parks – Conspicuous Consumption and Elite Status Rivalry', *Studies in the History of Gardens and Designed Landscapes*, 20 (2000), pp.206–228.

Granziera, P., 'Concept of the Garden in Pre-Hispanic Mexico', *Garden History*, 29:2 (Winter 2001), pp.185–213.

Granziera, P., 'Huaxtepec: The Sacred Garden of an Aztec Emperor', *Landscape Research*, 30:1 (2005), pp.81–107

Graulich, M., 'Aztec Festivals of the Rain Gods', *Indiana 12* (1992), pp. 21–54.

Taube, K., *The Major Gods of Ancient Yucatan (Pre-Columbian Art and Archaeology Studies)*, (1992), Harvard University Press.

# New beliefs

Dobransky, K. & Alan, G., 'The Native in the Garden: Floral Politics and Cultural Entrepreneurs', *Sociological Forum*, 21:4 (Dec 2006), pp.559–585.

ed. Marcus, C.C. & Bardnes, M., *Healing Gardens: Therapeutic Benefits and Design Recommendations* (1999), John Wiley & Sons.

Söderback, I., Söderström, M., Schälander, E., 'Horticultural therapy: the "healing garden" and gardening in rehabilitation measures at Danderyd hospital rehabilitation clinic, Sweden', *Pediatr Rehabil*, 7:4 (Oct–Dec 2004), pp.245–60.

Soulter-Brown, G., *Landscape and Urban Design for Health and Well-Being* (2014), Routledge.

Stigsdotter, U. & Grahn, P., 'What Makes a Garden a Healing Garden?', *Journal of Therapeutic Horticulture*, XIII (2002), pp.60–68.

# Index

Page numbers in *italic* refer to illustrations and their captions.

# Acknowledgements

An enormous 'thank you' is, as always, owed to Vibeke whose stoic patience and good humour eased the writing process and whose wise council doubtless improved the final product. Thank you too to Mirkko, a faithful companion throughout the many weeks I spent glued to my Mac.

A book has an author but the production of a book is a team effort and so I should like to express my thanks to all who have helped turn a concept into this lovely tome. Especially Helen Griffin at Frances Lincoln, Jane Crawley for her considered editing, Giulia Hetherington for her ingenious photo research, Philip Lewis for his artful lay out, Anna Watson and Jane Coulter.

The author and publisher are grateful for permission to quote from the following works:

'Aztec Festivals of the Rain Gods' by Michael Graulich, *Indiana*, 12 (1992), pp.37–38

*The Chinese Garden* by Maggie Keswick, Charles Jencks and Alison Harvey, Frances Lincoln Ltd (2003)

*Japanese Gardens* by Günter Nitschke, Taschen (2003)

# Picture credits